Cocktails
A-Go-Go

Cocktails

A-Go-Go

100 Swinging Drinks from Bahama Mamas to Salty Dogs

UNIVERSE

SUSAN WAGGONER AND ROBERT MARKEL

First published in the United States of America in 2003
by UNIVERSE PUBLISHING
A Division of Rizzoli International Publications, Inc.
300 Park Avenue South
New York, NY 10010

The authors would like to thank editor Chris Steighner and designer Kay Schuckhart for their
contributions to this book. Photos on pages 65 and 72 are reproduced courtesy of Diageo North
America, Stamford, CT. Photos on pages 5, 59–64, and 66 are by Ken Regan/Camera 5.
Photo on page 89 is reproduced courtesy of the Robert J. Markel Collection.

The authors and publisher of this book disclaim responsibility for
the improper use of any and all recipes and formulas herein. Text regarding
the use of alcohol, with the sole exception of the drink recipes provided,
is offered in the spirit of fun and is not meant to be taken literally.

Designed by Kay Schuckhart / Blond on Pond

2003 2004 2005 2006 2007 / 10 9 8 7 6 5 4 3 2 1

Printed in U.S.A.

ISBN: 0-7893-0846-0

Library of Congress Control Number: 2002112178

Contents

Bartender's Basics

Preparing a drink correctly and with care will always count for more with your guests than all the fancy glasses and gimmicky barware in the world. So let's start by focusing on what makes the perfect drink.

No matter what the cocktail is, there are three essential ingredients to keep in mind. They are:

- **COLD.** Unless a drink is specifically designed to be drunk at room temperature, it should be as cold as possible. This means using chilled glasses and chilled mixers (juice, soda, etc.). If you have several guests drinking the same cocktail, make drinks in batches rather than one at a time, as single drinks warm up more quickly.
- **FRESHNESS.** A drink should be served and drunk immediately after being made. If not, the delicately blended ingredients will begin to separate.
- **PROPERLY MEASURED INGREDIENTS.** Don't try to estimate how much of an ingredient you have added to the glass or the shaker — even a small miscalculation can alter the taste of a drink substantially, and the results are more likely to be a disappointment than a thrilling new discovery.

EQUIPMENT

You don't have to spend a lot of money to stock a bar adequately. As you go along, you will undoubtedly add to your store of glasses, accessories, spirits, liqueurs, and so on, but here is a list of basics to get you started.

BARWARE

When buying barware, we strongly urge you to avoid the cute in favor of the serviceable. A shaker of neon plastic shaped like a flying saucer may look irresistibly cool, but it may not give good results. The best shakers are glass or metal — materials which chill readily and will not conduct the warmth of your hands to the drink. Here is our list of items no good bar should be without:

- Shaker (which can double as a mixing glass).
- Strainer made to fit the shaker.
- Marked jigger or shot glass for measuring spirits.
- Corkscrew and bottle opener.
- Cutting board and paring knife.
- Ice bucket and tongs.
- Stirring spoon.
- Bar towels — clean, folded, and ready for service.
- Drink stirrers and toothpicks.
- Cocktail napkins.

GLASSES

Bars stock everything from brandy snifters to tiki mugs, but you can have an adequate home bar with just a few basic types.

- **WINE GLASS.** Basic stemmed wine glasses can do double duty for frozen blended drinks such as Grasshoppers and Margaritas.
- **COCKTAIL GLASS.** The classic stemmed "birdbath" glass is a must if you plan to prepare classic cocktails such as Martinis, Manhattans, and the like.
- **OLD FASHIONED GLASS.** This squat, straight-sided glass, which holds 8 to 10 ounces, is de rigueur for spirits served on the rocks, as its width allows every drop in the glass to come in contact with the chilling ice.
- **HIGHBALL GLASS.** Narrower and taller

than the Old Fashioned glass, this one is the choice for drinks that combine spirits with a nonalcoholic mixer.

- **COLLINS GLASS.** Similar to the highball glass in design, the Collins glass holds 10 to 12 ounces and is needed for drinks that have a greater volume of mixer. Many summertime drinks and tiki-era drinks fall into this category.
- **SHOT GLASS.** If you and your guests enjoy spirits straight up, you will need at least a few of these squat little glasses. A good shot glass should have a well-weighted bottom, to keep it from tipping over too easily.

WHAT WILL YOU HAVE TO DRINK?

Many people want to "be ready for anything" when it comes to stocking a home bar. News flash: You are *not* Vic of Trader Vic's or Harry of Harry's New York Bar. You are not even Joe down at the corner pub. Your friends won't expect you to make a Double Green Lizard Sake Sombrero with a twist of kiwi. Trying to cover all the bases is a good way to waste a lot of money, and you would be better off to begin by stocking a few high-quality basics and building up your selection gradually as you develop your own tastes and discover new favorites.

A good basic bar would include:

- Spirits
  - Gin
  - Vodka
  - Rum
  - Scotch
  - Blended whiskey
  - Sweet vermouth
  - Dry vermouth
  - Wine (one good red and one good white)

- Mixers and nonalcoholic beverages
  - Orange juice
  - Grapefruit juice
  - Tomato juice
  - Lemon-lime soda
  - Ginger ale
  - Cola
  - Club soda
  - Tonic water

- Condiments
  - Lemons, limes, and oranges
  - Rose's lime juice
  - Superfine sugar
  - Maraschino cherries
  - Angostura bitters
  - Worcestershire sauce
  - Tabasco
  - Cocktail olives
  - Cocktail onions

THE PERFECT COCKTAIL PARTY

Nothing is quite as splendidly retro as a cocktail party. They were de rigueur in the last half of the twentieth century, and we are pleased to see they're making a chic comeback in the twenty-first. If you want to give a successful party, here are some steps that will help ensure both you and your guests have a good time.

- **DEVELOP A DRINK MENU.** As we noted, trying to be prepared for all contingencies is not the way to go. For one thing, it will cost you an unnecessary amount of money. More important, trying to mix too many kinds of cocktails will create chaos behind the bar. It is better to select a menu of cocktails and prepare them well.

- **DEVELOP A FOOD MENU.** You should serve some form of food at a cocktail party — not because your guests will be ravenous, but because food is a good way to keep guests from going overboard with the alcohol. What you serve will depend on your budget, the crowd you've invited, and whether you want your party to be formal or casual. For an informal party, crackers, crudités, dips, and bowls of pretzels or popcorn are fine. The traditional food for a formal cocktail party is hors d'oeuvres, which can be anything from simple cheese-stuffed celery sticks to elaborate tempura on a stick. While cooked items are welcome, our best advice is to stick to hors d'oeuvres that can be prepared ahead of time and served at room temperature. The foods you choose don't need to be fancy, but they should be tasty as well as easy to eat while standing and conversing.

- **EXAMINE YOUR GUEST LIST.** Once you've developed both a drink and a food menu, look over your guest list again. Are the guests and the items you've selected a match? It is your responsibility to make sure that everyone, regardless of personal tastes, dietary restrictions, or other factors will find something acceptable to eat and drink at your party.

- **PLAN YOUR MUSIC.** Just as you have a food and drink menu, you should also plan a music menu. The music you choose should fit the tone of your cocktail party, be light and upbeat, and not be so loud or distracting that it will overwhelm your guests' conversation. If you don't have appropriate tapes or CDs, your library probably will, and you can check out a good selection without having to buy new discs.

- **THE DAY BEFORE THE PARTY . . .** At least one day before the party, do a final inventory. Do you have enough glasses (at least two for each person) and do you have drink stirrers and cocktail napkins to go with them? Do you have enough spirits, mixers, and food items? Will you have enough ice? (No matter how much ice you have, we suggest you lay in a few extra bags — it's inexpensive and will save the inconvenience of having to dash out for more.)

- **THE DAY OF THE PARTY . . .** Set up your station and look at it from a bartender's point of view. Where will the drinks be made? Is everything you will need on hand? Is it in an easy-to-get-to part of the room, or will it cause congestion? Now look at the room from your guests' points of view. Are there tables to set drinks on? Receptacles for crumpled cocktail napkins? Are there at least some chairs or conversation areas for those who may tire of standing?

- **A FEW HOURS BEFORE THE PARTY . . .** Are mixers such as soda and fruit juices chilled? How about your glasses? You can save time by preparing garnishes ahead of time — scraping citrus peels to cut into twists, draining olives and cherries and placing them in small cups, cutting slices of orange, lemon, and lime: all of these will keep perfectly well at room temperature under plastic wrap until your party is underway.

HOW MUCH WILL YOU NEED?

How much of any one item you need will depend on your guests' individual capacities, the length of the party, and the time of day and day of the week on which it is held (people drink more on weekend nights, for example). Here are some very general guidelines to follow. Please note that our chart assumes that each guest will choose one kind of drink and stick with it, rather than switching between, say, wine and mixed drinks.

BEVERAGES

Champagne	$1/2$ bottle per person
Wine	$2/3$ bottle per person
Liquor	$1/4$ fifth per person if drinking cocktails or on the rocks
	$1/3$ fifth per person if drinking shots

HORS D'OEUVRES

Here's a paradox for you: The larger the guest list, the more different types of hors d'oeuvres you should serve, but the fewer pieces you will need for each person. Why this is we aren't sure, but so many party planners have told us so that we take their word for it. Below is a very general guide to the number of types of hor d'oeuvres and the number of pieces you should plan for each person. Please note that "Hors d'oeuvres per person" means the total number they will consume, regardless of type. Personally, when it comes to food, we always prefer to err on the side of overestimating, as one of the perks of being a host is snacking on leftover hors d'oeuvres the day after the party.

Number of guests	Hors d'oeuvres per person	Different types
20 or fewer	5–6	6–7 different types
20–50	4–5	7–8 different types
50 or more	3–4	8–10 different types

The Cold War—The Very Cold War

"I never have more than one drink before dinner. But I do like that one to be large and very strong and very cold and very well-made."
— James Bond (David Niven) in Casino Royale, 1967

Even if you weren't around for the Cold War, chances are good you've still bumped up against its lingering cultural influences. And if you *were* around for those years — well, you can stop ducking and covering; the Russkies are our friends now. From the end of WW II through the fall of the Berlin Wall, the Cold War was a driving cultural force. Fallout shelters were fashionable; one Florida couple — Melvin and Maria Minnison — spent their two-week honeymoon in a shelter and emerged to find themselves surrounded by newspaper columnists, radio and television reporters, and photographers from *Life* magazine. School children practiced hiding under their desks (a surefire way to escape the ravages of a 50-megaton A-bomb), and adults debated the consequences of strontium 90 in the milk. Radio stations interrupted broadcasts frequently to check the Conelrad system and ran public service announcements informing citizens that "many millions" of Americans were still without fallout shelters. On television, Rocky and Bullwinkle foiled the plans of spies Boris and Natasha every Saturday morning, while *Mad* magazine's "Spy vs. Spy" comic strip delivered a surprisingly sophisticated take on the absurdity of mutually assured destruction. Adult TV viewers could indulge in *The Man from U.N.C.L.E.*, *I Spy*, or, for laughs, *Get Smart*. As novels, Fletcher Knebel's *Seven Days in May* and Nevil Shute's *On the Beach* spent weeks on the bestseller lists before their film versions scared millions of moviegoers out of their wits. And for every *Failsafe* and *Dr. Strangelove*, there were dozens of nuclear-inspired B-movies, from *Invasion USA* to *The Day the World Ended* and *Panic in the Year Zero*.

Vesper

Though James Bond is most often associated with Martinis, his drink of choice in *Casino Royale* is an invention all his own: one he names "The Vesper" in tribute to his foil, a lushly blonde double agent. Unfortunately, Vesper commits suicide before the movie's end, and Bond (seen below as played by Sean Connery) thereafter switches to Martinis. But the drink he created is well worth remembering — and drinking again. Like the double agent, this drink is a lalapalooza, and one is probably too much to handle.

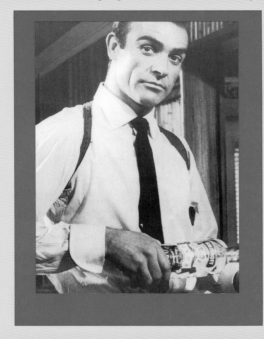

3 ounces gin
1 ounce vodka
$\frac{1}{2}$ ounce blonde Lillet

Place ingredients in a cocktail shaker with cracked ice. Shake and strain into a chilled cocktail glass. Bond liked his with a long, "large, thin slice of lemon peel," but we prefer ours as it was served at the Rainbow Room in New York, with a vibrant twist of orange peel.

"Although means of heating food should be available in the shelter, precooked foods and those that require little or no heating before eating should be chosen in preference to other foods. . . . Can and bottle openers should not be forgotten!"
— Personal and Family Survival, Civil Defense Manual SM 3-11, 1963

Oddly enough, fallout-shelter manuals never recommended stocking two indispensable staples of the era — booze and cigarettes. It was a nervous time, and, not surprisingly, people drank and smoked with abandon. Cigarettes did not yet carry warning labels, and TV comics made insouciant references to the cocktails they consumed. Drinking was a chic adult activity, something one dressed up for and took pains to do correctly, in a swank lounge or at a cocktail party. Symbols of the chic style of imbibing were everywhere, and nowhere more in evidence than at the movies, in the character of James Bond, the archetype of Cold War cool.

Silver Bullet

Although this drink was invented in the 1930s, it became popular again during the Cold War, when it was a mark of sophistication to sip cocktails made with "exotic" foreign spirits. We give the original recipe below, although over the last few decades the vodka variation has become the more popular version of the drink.

2 ounces gin
1 ounce kummel
1 ounce freshly squeezed lemon juice

Shake ingredients with cracked ice in a cocktail shaker. Strain into a chilled cocktail glass.

VARIATION: VODKA SILVER BULLET. Replace gin with 1½ ounces vodka, omit lemon juice, and make as described above.

Kamikaze

Americans may have been locked in an arms race with the Russians, but that didn't prevent them from inventing — or, in this case, reinventing — any number of vodka-based drinks. The Kamikaze is actually a modernized version of an earlier cocktail known as the Balalaika, which has lemon juice instead of lime.

1 ounce vodka

1 ounce triple sec

1 ounce freshly squeezed lime juice

Combine ingredients in a mixing glass with cracked ice. Stir, then strain into a chilled cocktail glass.

Cape Codder

Though dipped in the glamour of the Kennedys' summer retreat, this drink owes more to the improvement of the interstate highway system. Long-distance trucking, improvements in frozen-food technology, and other innovations made for a greater availability of food products than ever before. One previously exotic item, cranberry juice, soon made its way to the cocktail circuit.

1½ ounces vodka

4 ounces cranberry juice

Dash of lime juice

1 teaspoon simple syrup (optional)

Place all ingredients in a shaker with cracked ice. Shake and strain into a chilled cocktail glass.

Golden Cadillac

Like spiked heels and cocktail parties, after-dinner drinks were still chic in the 1960s. Galliano, an herb-and-spice liqueur, was a perfect base around which to build new aperitifs. Galliano, which made its American debut in 1960, was imported from Italy, which gave it the exotic twist of being foreign and thrillingly sophisticated. Americans lost no time in crafting it into a drink that epitomized a cultural icon particularly their own — the huge and showy luxury car.

2 ounces Galliano
1 ounce white crème de cacao
1 ounce cream

Combine all ingredients in a cocktail shaker with cracked ice, shake briskly, and strain into a chilled cocktail glass. Do not garnish — the lovely golden hue of this drink provides all the visual allure needed.

VARIATION: VELVET HAMMER. Actually, the Velvet Hammer predates the Golden Cadillac and may well have served as its inspiration. To make a Velvet Hammer, follow the recipe and method above but replace the 2 ounces of Galliano with 1 ounce of Cointreau.

Golden Dream

Here's another beautiful drink from the 1960s, the color of which suggests the deep golden rays of sunrise and sunset. Galliano was dedicated by its nineteenth-century Italian inventor to the gold rush–inspired dreams of California in particular and the United States in general. In the serenity this drink imparts, one can still taste the tranquility of suburbia and the giddy prosperity of middle-class America. Have one on your patio and you'll know why the Kennedy years are so fondly remembered.

1 1/2 ounces Galliano
1 ounce Cointreau
1 ounce orange juice
1/2 tablespoon cream

Combine all ingredients in a cocktail shaker with cracked ice, shake, and strain into a chilled cocktail glass. Do not garnish.

Blend-O-Rama

Rudy Vallee? Fred Waring and the Pennsylvanians? Purveyors of yesterday's music they may have been, but they're also unsung heroes in any bartender's hall of fame. Their visionary efforts led to a revolution in the art of mixology, giving us some of our favorite contemporary classics.

It all began long ago, in a dressing room far, far away. In the early 1930s, Fred Waring was a well-known music producer and entrepreneur. A former Penn State engineering student, he was also a lover of gadgets, innovations, and inventions. One night after Waring finished a radio broadcast from New York's Vanderbilt Theater, an inventor named Fred Osius talked his way backstage and gained access to his dressing room. Osius believed Waring was the perfect source for funding for his newest idea, a contraption that would emulsify food. Intrigued by the idea, Waring not only provided funding, but was responsible for several improvements in the design itself. The ultimate result was a prototype of what would become the Waring Blendor, which burst upon an unwitting public in 1938.

It's one thing to lead a horse to water, another to make it drink — and in this case the horse was the public. No one seemed quite as enamored of the gadget as Waring himself was, and the least enamored of all was Waring's choral

Frozen Daiquiri

Daiquiris have been around since the turn of the century, but they got a big boost in popularity in the 1960s, when John Fitzgerald Kennedy became president. After the sedate and stodgy Eisenhower era, the Kennedy White House glowed with youth and glamour, and when word got out that the Daiquiri was the president's cocktail of choice, it became the "in" drink of the era.

1½ ounces light rum
Juice of 1½ limes (approximately 1½ ounces)
1 teaspoon sugar
1 cup cracked ice

Combine ingredients in blender and whir just until smooth. While this recipe can be multiplied to make several drinks at once, don't make more than will be served immediately, as the delight of a Frozen Daiquiri is its soft, fresh slushiness. Garnish with a thin slice of lime if you like.

VARIATION: To make a traditional Daiquiri, place lime juice in a cocktail shaker. Add sugar and stir until dissolved. Add other ingredients, shake briefly, and strain into a cocktail glass. A traditional Daiquiri needs no garnish, but a thin slice of lime or a twist of lemon may be used.

group, the Pennsylvanians. On tour, Waring had a special traveling trunk made for his beloved blender. He believed the invention would revolutionize the art of gastronomy and, eager to put his theory to work, chased after members of his company with tumblers full of pulverized food. From green beans to cranberries to sauerkraut, nothing was safe from the whirling blades of the blender.

"At first we considered the whole affair a harmless foible — the sort of squirrelly therapy one expects a man of certain genius to contrive for his own amusement."
—Ferne Buckner, Member of the Pennsylvanians

Revolt was in the air. Members of the Pennsylvanians let it be known that if they were presented with one more concoction of buttermilk and borscht puree, they'd leave the tour. In a last-ditch effort to put his project across, Waring changed strategies. A nondrinker himself, Waring knew that his troupe enjoyed their cocktails. Why not put his invention to work behind the bar? According to Ferne Buckner, who was with the Pennsylvanians at the time, the first drink ever concocted in the blender was a Frozen Daiquiri. The cocktail, which took 10 or 15 minutes to prepare by hand, was whirred to icy perfection in a matter of minutes. Pennsylvanians who had so recently threatened to flee now lined up for samples.

Having discovered the hook needed to engage the public's attention, Waring now stepped up his sales efforts. Wherever the Pennsylvanians played, Waring took his machine to the leading department store and put on a demonstration for the buyers. He also put on demonstrations for friends. Upon learning that the popular crooner Rudy Vallee was a Frozen Daiquiri fanatic, Waring invited Vallee to stop by his dressing room for a chat. Vallee was on a tight schedule, about to catch a return trip to Hollywood, and when Waring offered to make him a drink, Vallee insisted that he didn't have time. Over the singer's objections, Waring began dumping the contents of Vallee's favorite drink — a Strawberry Daiquiri — into the blender, and in one minute presented him with a perfect cocktail. After a single sip, Vallee told Waring he wanted to be his agent, and Waring allowed him to return to Hollywood with the gadget.

Frozen Strawberry Daiquiri

1 1/2 ounces light rum
Juice of 1 lime
   (approximately 1 ounce)
1 teaspoon sugar
6 large strawberries
   (fresh or frozen)
1/2 cup cracked ice

**Make as Frozen Daiquiri, page 19.
Garnish with a large strawberry.**

Frozen Banana Daiquiri

1 1/2 ounces light rum
1 tablespoon fresh lime juice
1 tablespoon milk or cream
1/3 banana, broken into chunks
1/2 cup cracked ice
Make as Frozen Daiquiri, page 19.

Frozen Pineapple Daiquiri

2 ounces light rum
1/2 ounce Cointreau
3 ounces pineapple juice
Dash of freshly squeezed
   lime juice
**Make as Frozen Daiquiri,
   page 19.**

Whether Waring actually expected Vallee to follow through with his plan is unknown, but within a few weeks Vallee called Waring to inform him that sales were brisk.

Vallee, Waring learned, had an almost perfect sales technique. After finishing his performance for the evening, Vallee would wander into a bar and order a Frozen Daiquiri. When the bartenders frowned over the effort it took to make the drink, Vallee would innocently ask, "Don't you have a Waring mixer?" to the inevitable response of "What's a Waring mixer?" Vallee would produce the blender, plug it in behind the bar, and within minutes mix a pitcher of Frozen

Brandy Alexander

More than 40 years after it was made, Edward Blake's *The Days of Wine and Roses* remains as gripping a picture of alcoholism as was ever crafted. Anyone who has seen the film may well remember that lovely Lee Remick's character didn't begin her descent with raw gin or even the proverbial Martini, but with the Brandy Alexander — a good reason never to have more than one of these seductive little sippers.

1 ounce brandy
1 ounce crème de cacao
1 ounce heavy cream
1/2 cup cracked ice

Combine all ingredients in blender, whir for about half a minute, and serve immediately. This recipe can be increased to make multiple drinks, but, as with all frozen drinks, do not make more than will be served at once. Garnish if you like with a light dusting of cocoa powder, cinnamon, or nutmeg.

VARIATION: For a creamier treat, replace the heavy cream and ice with 3/4 cup ice cream.

Daiquiris. Before he left the establishment, he'd invariably have written an order for one or more of the appliances. By the end of 1938, more than 35,000 blenders had been sold.

Just as Waring's machine was gaining a solid foothold, World War II intervened. The scarcity of materials needed for the war effort called a halt to mass production, and Waring sold his license to a parent manufacturing company. Although the blender continued to be used in scientific venues such as hospitals and research labs, it ceased to be the going concern it once had been. The blender's real era of popularity did not begin until well after World War II, when a number of happy factors converged to make it one of the most popular appliances in history.

The American kitchen before 1950 was largely an appliance wasteland. Aside from the toaster, its counters were more or less bare. But after the war, when suburbs began to boom all over the country, more couples found themselves in possession of more counter space and more money to spend filling that counter space than ever before. Happily, the war effort left us with a lot of first-class engineers, many of whom found jobs inventing coffee makers, electric mixers, and all sorts of other plug-in delights. It was only a matter of time until someone figured out that the blender, once a piece of "professional" equipment, could be manufactured for home use. Soon people were blending away, and a whole new generation of drinks became popular. Frozen drinks for Mom and Dad as they lounged on their newly flagstoned patio, malts and milkshakes for the kids to drink with the burgers Dad was grilling — could anything be more perfectly designed for the new, efficient, fully equipped American hearth? The blender had come into its own at last.

Grasshopper

1 ounce crème de menthe
1 ounce white crème de cacao
1 ounce heavy cream
1/2 cup cracked ice

Combine all ingredients in blender, whir for about half a minute, and serve immediately. This recipe can be increased to make multiple drinks, but, as with all frozen drinks, do not make more than will be served at once. Garnish if you like with a fresh mint leaf or dusting of cocoa powder.

VARIATION: As with the Brandy Alexander, heavy cream and ice may be replaced with 3/4 cup ice cream.

VARIATION: VODKA GRASSHOPPER. If you'd like your Grasshopper to have a bit more kick, add 1 ounce of vodka to make a Vodka Grasshopper — and leave the ice cream alone.

VARIATION: MEXICAN GRASSHOPPER. Substitute 1 ounce of coffee liqueur for the crème de cacao.

Lounge Lizards

Zebra- and leopard-print upholstery, plenty of ashtrays, colored aluminum bowls filled with cocktail peanuts, dim lighting, and an overall absence of feminine frills — it's the height of lounge luxe, and you'd be surprised how many people are re-creating it in their own home bars.

If you're one of these, you could do no better than to study Las Vegas for inspiration. No, not the new family-friendly Vegas with reconstructed Eiffel Towers and imported bits of London Bridge. We mean the *old* Vegas, where the Rat Pack performed nightly, where steaks were consumed without a thought about cholesterol counts, and where cigarettes were smoked with glorious abandon.

Carved out of the desert, Las Vegas's first generation of modest hotels and casinos gave way, in the 1950s and 1960s, to a second generation of audaciously large and flashy resorts. The Sands, the Sahara, the Desert Inn, the Stardust, the Tropicana — all filled the night sky with bursts of neon and the glimmer of excitement. To lure customers into their casinos, most hotels had swank lounges where, for the price of a drink, patrons could watch live entertainment at any hour of the day or night. Beyond the lounges were the larger showrooms, where one could drink, dine, and see world-famous performers. As the nightclub scene was dying elsewhere in America, Las Vegas roared to life, and many nightclub headliners began appearing in Vegas on a regular basis. The

Copa Room at the Sands was a particular favorite, and the infamous Rat Pack (Frank Sinatra, Dean Martin, Peter Lawford, Joey Bishop, and Sammy Davis Jr.) performed there for years before switching to Caesar's Palace.

"You're not drunk if you can lie on the floor without holding on."
— Dean Martin

In addition to singers and comics, there were dancing girls aplenty, and virtually every club worth its salt had a spectacular chorus line. The Lido de Paris performed at the Stardust from 1960 through 1991, the Folies Bergère was stationed at the Tropicana, and at the Dunes, the girls of the Minsky's Follies were the first to appear topless.

Vegas in the 1960s was the height of lounge culture. It may not have been politically correct, or even healthy, but it was one *heck* of a good time. And while we don't endorse all-night drinking and gambling sessions, we do endorse the spirit of the place.

The Original Jack Daniels Test Pilot

Jack Daniels was Frank Sinatra's drink of choice, and he never traveled without several cases of the stuff. When a physician once asked him how many drinks he had per day, Sinatra answered, "about 36," based on the number of pours he got out of the fifth he handily put away between dawn and dusk (or dusk and dawn, depending on how the day was going). Although the alarmed physician begged him to cut back, Sinatra refused. According to some accounts, he even went so far as to change doctors.

Sinatra was as precise about how his drink should be made as he was about everything else, from the length of his shirt cuffs to the notes of a Nelson Riddle arrangement. To make the drink his way, start with a traditional, heavy-bottomed Old Fashioned glass. Add three to four ice cubes and two fingers (1 ounce) of Jack Daniels. Top off with plain water. Don't drink immediately; give the booze and the water a chance to mingle with the ice's chill.

Presenting the world's finest entertainment

Highballs

No-frills drinks are the hallmark of lounge culture — no paper umbrellas or fruit juice drinks here. Which makes this a good time to offer a refresher course on the classic Highball. This drink, which combines $1^1/_2$ ounces of liquor with a mixer, should be made in a Highball glass filled with ice. Too many people, we've noticed, ruin the Highball by overmixing. It's best to remember that this isn't a blended drink — when you sip it, you should taste different gradations of the ingredients. Moreover, overmixing will dissipate the carbonation and lessen the drink's fresh fizz. To make a proper Highball, fill the glass to the top with ice, pour the spirits over the ice cubes, add the mixer, and stir only once or twice. Although these drinks were invented when members of the Rat Pack were still in knee pants, they prevailed as some of the most popular drinks of the lounge era.

- **RUM AND COKE.** Note that it isn't called "Rum and Cola," and for a very good reason. For this cocktail, only use the real thing.
- **SEVEN AND SEVEN.** Seagram's 7-Crown whiskey and lemon-lime soda.
- **BOURBON AND BRANCH.** Bourbon and water.
- **SCOTCH AND SODA.** Leave the lemon peel at home — this sophisticated Highball never takes a garnish — just pure Scotch and club soda, baby.
- **GIN AND TONIC.** Begin by rubbing the rim of the glass with a wedge of fresh lime. This Highball is best if you don't stir it at all.
- **VODKA AND TONIC.** Vodka and tonic water with a wedge of lemon or lime.
- **GIN CHILLER OR VODKA CHILLER.** Gin (or vodka) with ginger ale, garnished with a wedge of lime.

Old Fashioned

Only slightly more difficult to make than a simple Highball, the Old Fashioned is another classic that survived well into the lounge era. Although the original drink was made with rye, bourbon was the standard base by the 1960s.

2 ounces bourbon
1 teaspoon sugar (or 1 lump)
Splash of water
2 dashes Angostura bitters
Orange wedge
Maraschino cherry

Place sugar, water, and bitters in the bottom of an Old Fashioned glass and stir until sugar is dissolved. Add the orange and the cherry. Using a muddler or the back of a heavy spoon, crush lightly to make a rough paste. Add the spirits. Fill with as many ice cubes as the glass will take. Stir.

Music for Show
and Dancing by
CARLTON HAYES
AND HIS ORCHESTRA

Pink Lady

You don't expect those ladies in their spiked heels, gold lamé, and furs to knock back Bourbons on the Rocks, do you? One of the charming features of the lounge era was that, while it was perfectly acceptable for a woman to order a Martini, there were also still such things as "girl" drinks and "boy" drinks. The Pink Lady, below, and her sister, the White Lady, right, are two of our favorites.

1 ounce gin
1/2 ounce lemon juice
1/2 ounce grenadine
1 ounce cream

Place all ingredients in a shaker with cracked ice. Shake and strain into a chilled cocktail glass.

White Lady

1 1/2 ounces gin
3/4 ounce lemon juice
3/4 ounce Cointreau

Place all ingredients in a shaker with cracked ice. Shake and strain into a chilled cocktail glass.

SHOW TIMES
8:15 P. M. and
12 Midnight
Friday Also, 2:15 A.M.

Bloody Caesar

According to the story, Tony Bennett was performing in Vegas when, one night, he discovered he'd had one too many and asked the Caesar's Palace bartender to fix him up with something stabilizing. The bartender came up with this, which, given what we've heard of Vegas, no doubt passed as a well-balanced meal.

1 1/2 ounces vodka
5 ounces clamato juice (a combination of tomato and clam juices)
1 tablespoon freshly squeezed lemon juice
2 dashes of Worcestershire sauce
Dash of Tabasco sauce
Pinch of celery salt
Pinch of black pepper

Fill a Highball glass almost to the top with ice. Add clamato and lemon juices. Pour in vodka. Add Worcestershire, Tabasco, celery, salt, and pepper. Stir. Garnish with a wedge of lime.

Bossa Nova

South American rhythms were big in the 1960s, and it isn't surprising that a cocktail was created to honor the Brazilian beat that sounded intimate and oh-so-modern when played in the wee hours of the morning. The original drink used a dash of raw egg white, which, for safety reasons, we've taken the liberty of replacing with a bit of cream. Actually, we think it makes the drink taste even better.

1 ounce Galliano
1 ounce white rum
1/2 ounce apricot brandy

1/2 ounce lemon juice
1 ounce pineapple juice
Dash of cream

Fill a cocktail shaker with cracked ice and add all the ingredients. Shake and strain into a chilled cocktail glass. Garnish with a sprig of mint.

Godfather

If you know your *Godfather* movies, it will come as no surprise that the mob had a certain hand in the creation of Las Vegas. So where better to sip this drink?

1¹⁄₂ ounces Scotch
³⁄₄ ounce amaretto

Fill an Old Fashioned glass with ice. Add Scotch and amaretto and stir. Do not garnish.
VARIATION: GODMOTHER. Make as you would a Godfather, using vodka in place of Scotch.
VARIATION: GODCHILD. We've seen many versions of the Godchild, using everything from bourbon to vodka to brandy in place of the Godfather's Scotch, and adding 1¹⁄₂ ounces of cream.

31

Surfin' USA

I f you had landed without a map almost anywhere in the United States in the early 1960s, you might have decided you were in an island country whose sand-swept beaches must surely be just a few miles distant.

Surfing originated in Hawaii more than five hundred years ago and, for most of those centuries, it was a well-kept secret. Then America acquired Hawaii and, with the tropical territory headed for statehood, the mainland took to the sport in a big way. Oblivious to the fact that most of the country is in the Northern Hemisphere and even more of it is land-locked, American teens from Fargo to Phoenix spent the early 1960s listening to Beach Boys music and watching Annette Funicello, Frankie Avalon, Sandra Dee, and James Darren cavort through a host of beach movies. And long before she was *Sybil* or even *The Flying Nun,* Sally Field was *Gidget* in the TV version of the movie role. You have to hand it to them — it takes real esprit to live the surfin' lifestyle when the biggest wave you see is whatever the motorboats kick up at the lake.

Harvey Wallbanger

One of the most enduring bits of surf culture is the Harvey Wallbanger. According to lore, it was invented by a surfer, Harvey, to salve his dented pride after wiping out in a surf championship. The scene allegedly occurred in Pancho's, a Manhattan Beach, California, bar favored by the surfing set. Still sorrowing over the lost championship, Harvey got up after several of these concoctions and slammed his head into a wall. Friends intervened to prevent permanent damage, but Harvey's drink of choice bears the name to this day.

1 1/2 ounces vodka
4 to 6 ounces orange juice
1/2 ounce Galliano

Place several ice cubes in a Collins glass. Add vodka, then orange juice, and stir well. Float the Galliano on top.

SANGRIA

Sangria, the wine punch of Spanish origin, was a popular drink of the beach era — perhaps because it was easy to mix in large quantities. Early recipes for Sangria usually combine wine, fruit, and spirits. Later versions have increased the fruit flavors and, in some cases, eliminated the spirits. This is fine, and Sangria is generally a "free-form" experience, with no two recipes being exactly alike. But we caution against Sangria that is too sweet — we've had some in which the dominant taste is best described as "bubble gum." A good Sangria should have sharp notes as well as sweet. The recipes below can be increased proportionately to serve more guests.

Quick Sangria

1 bottle red wine
1 1/2 ounces freshly squeezed lime juice
3 ounces rum
Assorted fresh fruits

Mix first three ingredients several hours ahead of serving time and chill in the refrigerator. (If you can chill overnight, so much the better.) To serve, slice fruit as desired and place with a generous amount of ice and Sangria in a chilled pitcher. Typical fruits include oranges, lemons, limes, peaches, nectarines, apples, pineapple, and mangoes.

"Bring me my pendulum, kiddies.
I feel like swinging!"
— Big Daddy (Vincent Price) in
Beach Party, 1963

SURF-O-RAMA

Want to relive those carefree days on the beach? Rent one of the beachy classics below. How did those girls keep their teased hair so neat in all that humidity?

- **GIDGET** (1959). **Stars:** Sandra Dee, James Darren. **Plot:** Gidget's heart is torn between a muscular surfer and an endearing beach bum.
- **GIDGET GOES HAWAIIAN** (1961). **Stars:** Deborah Walley, James Darren. **Odd cameo:** Carl Reiner. **Plot:** Gidget flees to Hawaii after a bad breakup with Moondoggie. Of course, he follows.
- **BEACH PARTY** (1963). **Stars:** Annette Funicello, Frankie Avalon. **Odd cameos:** Dorothy Malone, Morey Amsterdam. **Plot:** An anthropologist studying the mating habits of teens stumbles across Annette, Frankie, and their band of friends.
- **MUSCLE BEACH PARTY** (1964). **Stars:** Annette Funicello, Frankie Avalon. **Odd cameo:** Buddy Hackett. **Plot:** Beach bunnies battle body builders for sandy turf — until a fortuitous recording contract makes everyone the best of friends.
- **BIKINI BEACH** (1964). **Stars:** Annette Funicello, Frankie Avalon. **Odd cameo:** Don Rickles. **Plot:** Frankie Avalon plays a dual role, appearing as Annette's boyfriend and as a British rock star known as "The Potato Bug."
- **BEACH BLANKET BINGO** (1965). **Stars:** Annette Funicello, Frankie Avalon. **Odd cameo:** Paul Lynde. **Plot:** A runaway pop singing star lands smack-dab in the middle of Annette and Frankie's beach.
- **HOW TO STUFF A WILD BIKINI** (1965). **Stars:** Annette Funicello, Dwayne Hickman. **Odd cameos:** Mickey Rooney, Buster Keaton. **Plot:** To make sure Annette remains faithful while he's away on active duty, boyfriend Frankie sends a witch doctor to keep the boys at bay.

36

Brandied Sangria

1 bottle red wine
1 1/2 ounces curaçao
2 tablespoons superfine sugar
1/2 orange, thinly sliced
1/2 lemon, thinly sliced
1 1/2 ounces brandy
16 ounces club soda

Combine wine, curaçao, sugar, and fruit slices. Stir to dissolve sugar and chill in refrigerator several hours or overnight. Shortly before serving, add brandy. Immediately before serving, add club soda and a generous amount of ice. Adding brandied fruit, such as peaches or cherries, is also a nice touch.

Mexican Spiced Sangria

1 bottle red wine

4 ounces tequila

2 ounces ounces curaçao

1 orange, thinly sliced

1 lemon, thinly sliced

1 lime, thinly sliced

2 or 3 cinnamon sticks, tied in a bundle

2 peaches, peeled, cut in halves, and studded with cloves

Combine wine, tequila, curaçao, and citrus slices. Chill in refrigerator several hours or overnight. Shortly before serving, pour into pitcher with a generous amount of ice. Add peach halves and cinnamon sticks.

VARIATION: For a sparkling Sangria, you may add 16 ounces of club soda or sparkling wine.

TIP:

When making Sangria or any other type of punch, you can avoid the problem of rapidly melting ice that causes dilution by using large blocks of ice (freeze water in one- or two-cup plastic containers, for example) or by making your ice cubes out of nonalcoholic ingredients you plan to add, such as fruit juice or club soda.

Get Out Your Tiki Torches

Strange as it may seem today, there was a time when it seemed perfectly natural to drive through a sub-zero January night and see, between whipping bursts of snow, the incongruous flames of sputtering torches, alerting you to the fact that you'd arrived at the Tiki Village apartment complex or the Bali Bali Room Polynesian restaurant. Those torches were a message to come on in, peel off your scarf, gloves, parka, and boots; have a drink in a coconut-shaped ceramic cup; relax and forget the impending blizzard outside. In other words — go tiki!

"I like rum. I like the drinks it makes and everything about it."
— Trader Vic Bergeron

In the 1960s, America and much of the world was in the grip of tiki-mania. The proliferation of tiki restaurants, bars, and even apartment complexes, like the interweaving of tiki elements into the culture, was the culmination of events that had begun more than a generation earlier.

TIKI TIMELINE

- **1920–1933 PROHIBITION.** When liquor becomes illegal in the U.S., bon vivants go overseas, many to Singapore and similarly exotic Pacific ports. Among the wanderers is Charles Baker, who collects and eventually publishes recipes for many tropical cocktails.

- **1932 HINKY DINK'S.** Restaurateur Victor Bergeron opens Hinky Dink's in Oakland, California. The menu, a mix of Chinese, Japanese, and Tahitian dishes, offers Americans their first taste of the Pacific.

- **1933 PROHIBITION REPEALED.** Prohibition may have ended in America, but the Depression hasn't. As a result, rum, the least expensive spirit, enjoys a wild surge in popularity.

- **1934 DON THE BEACHCOMBER.** Ernest Beaumont-Gantt opens his famous Hollywood restaurant, drawing on tropical themes from the Pacific as well as Jamaica, which he had visited in his youth. The colorful decorations and potent rum cocktails make the place an ideal escape from the Depression raging outside — and an instant hit with fun-seekers.

- **1936 TRADER VIC'S.** Bergeron changes the name of his restaurant from Hinky Dink's to Trader Vic's. Bergeron is a colorful character and master mixologist who soon becomes famous for his original and creative tropical cocktails.

- **1941–1945 WORLD WAR II.** America enters the war against Japan and the Axis. As a result, thousands of Americans see active duty in the Pacific.

- **1947 JAMES MICHENER'S *TALES OF THE SOUTH PACIFIC*.** Drawing on his own experiences during the war, Michener writes his first bestseller.

- **1949 RODGERS AND HAMMERSTEIN'S *SOUTH PACIFIC*.** The musical based on Michener's book opens on Broadway, feeding the war-nostalgia boom and offering up visions of a Polynesian paradise.

- **1950 *KON-TIKI*.** Norwegian adventurer Thor Heyerdahl publishes a book based on his experiences rafting from Peru to Polynesia.

- **1956–1959 *BOLD JOURNEY*.** This odd TV travelogue program aired home movies of people who'd traveled to distant locales — Pacific adventures were often featured, further fueling the appetite for the exotic tropical experience.

- **1959 HAWAII.** At last, America has its own island paradise.

- **1959 *HAWAII*.** James Michener's newest saga becomes an instant bestseller.

- **1960S GENERALIZED HAWAII-MANIA.** Americans embrace their new state with gusto. Honolulu becomes a popular vacation destination. On the mainland, reasonable-minded women decide that it's perfectly OK to appear in public in a mumu. The luau is the party hit of the decade.

- **1962 *BLUE HAWAII*.** Elvis's new movie, and the title song to go with it, sets the stage for music with palm-tree flair.

- **1966 DON HO.** Native Hawaiian singer Don Ho sings "Tiny Bubbles" at the Coconut Grove in L.A. and becomes a national sensation.

- **1970S CARIBBEAN CULTURE.** Immigrants from the Caribbean stream into America, while more and more Americans vacation in the Bahamas, Jamaica, Puerto Rico, and other nearby tropical zones. "Tiki" cocktails are no longer confined to Singapore Slings and Samoan Fog Cutters — Bahama Mamas and Piña Coladas are added to the mix.

LET'S HAVE A LUAU

Nothing says *tiki* like a good luau, and few theme parties are as fun, flexible, or easy to stage. If you've never hosted a luau or been to one, don't miss your chance — get out your leis, tuck an orchid behind your ear, and get in the spirit. Here are some pointers for your party.

DRESS

Encourage your guests to dress the part. Almost everyone has something in the closet that can rise to the occasion — flip-flops, beach cover-ups, floral prints, and batik fabric are perfect. Sarongs, sundresses, paraeos, and mumus are great for women, or halter tops paired with shorts or wraparound skirts. For men, Hawaiian shirts, shorts, jams, and other "beachcomber" items work just fine. As the host, you'll want to have leis of plastic or paper flowers on hand for your guests, as well as anklets and wrist bands of artificial flowers for the women.

LOCALE

The great thing about a luau is that you can have one almost anywhere. While the classic luau is held outdoors, you can have just as much fun in a suburban basement decorated for the occasion, and not having space for a barbecue pit shouldn't deter you — there are plenty of other authentic foods you can serve.

DECORATIONS

Decoration is a must for a good luau, as part of the fun is the mix of bright, exciting colors. You can make your own decorations or purchase inexpensive ones. If your local party store fails you, we found a number of suppliers on the Internet who specialize in tropical party decor and ship at reasonable rates. Exposed beams and rafters? Hang up some fishnets or colorful paper parrots, wind chimes, and paper lanterns. Support poles holding up the beams? Turn them into fake palm trees. Dull, boring walls? Make your own tiki masks or totems out of brown paper or try a garland of paper pineapples. Lawn flamingos and shells are great to scatter around, as are votive candles scented with coconut, pineapple, gardenia, or other tropical scents. If candles present a safety hazard, strings of mini-lights add a festive and romantic touch. Indoors or out, card tables can be covered with bamboo mats or trimmed with raffia hula skirts. Glass bowls filled with water and floating candles or a few exotic blossoms (real or fake) make good table decorations, as do edible centerpieces such as hollowed-out melons or pineapples filled with fresh fruits.

If you are having your party outdoors, invest in a few tiki torches — not only are they festive, they help keep the insects at bay.

SERVINGWARE

So many paper plates, napkins, and tablecloths come in tropical themes that it seems a shame to use real dishes — so save yourself the trouble of a big cleanup and buy as many disposable items as you can. If you really want to splurge, spend your money on fun barware — tiki mugs and ceramic coconuts are traditional and easy to find. If you don't want to carry things quite that far, go for less expensive items like palm and flamingo swizzle sticks, brightly colored straws, paper umbrellas, or the small, brightly colored plastic toys (mermaids, elephants, squids, monkeys, etc.) now sold to garnish glasses with.

FOOD

Most people think of roast pork as the "traditional" luau dish, and it certainly is, but there are many other equally authentic dishes that can be served. Remember that Hawaii is a blend of many different cultures — Chinese, Japanese, Korean, Portuguese, Filipino, Samoan, Tahitian, American, and now even Caribbean and African, just to name a few. A menu that includes dishes representing several of these different cuisines isn't just permitted, it's encouraged, as are imaginative reinterpretations of traditional favorites. (This is one reason why fried rice in Hawaii almost invariably includes Spam!)

When it comes to food, you can do almost anything you want with your luau — serve a full, multicourse meal or just appetizers; please tailgating, meat-eater types or health-minded vegetarians; satisfy spice lovers as well as those who are sensitive to salt, spices, and other seasonings.

APPETIZERS: Chinese spareribs, egg rolls, spring rolls, coconut shrimp, chicken wings, dumplings, wonton crisps.

MAIN DISHES: Stir fry, kebabs, teriyaki, steamed or grilled whole fish, shrimp, scallops, roast pork, glazed ham, sweet-and-sour dishes, honey chicken, tempura, Korean short ribs, curry, sushi.

SIDE DISHES: Steamed rice, fried rice, coconut rice, sticky rice, macaroni salad, sesame noodles, pad thai, kim chee, Hawaiian bread, pita bread, rice crackers, beans and rice, grilled vegetables, roasted sweet potatoes, stir-fried or sauteed broccoli or string beans, snow peas, edamame, grilled tofu, sliced fresh fruit.

SALADS: Mixed greens, fruit salads, sprouts, coleslaw.

DESSERTS: Grilled pineapple, almond cookies, fortune cookies, pineapple carrot cake, coconut or mango sorbet, fruit sherbet.

ACTIVITIES

Aside from the meal, music and dancing are definite luau high points. In Hawaii, almost every tourist luau includes a hula demonstration put on by native dancers. But why just watch when you can participate? Hire an instructor to teach you and your guests to do this beautifully expressive dance, or, at the very least, get some music and an instruction book and give it a try. More raucous is the limbo, where dancers compete to dance beneath a bar that is gradually lowered until all but the final winner is eliminated. Almost any music store will have appropriate CDs, or you can check out the collection at your local library.

The Dinklers present LUAU

AMERICA'S MOST EXOTIC, EXCITING, SENSATIONAL RESTAURANT

Samoan Fog Cutter

This is another drink that existed back in the 1930s, then vanished — only to be rediscovered and enjoyed as a hip new drink during the tiki craze of the 1960s.

2 ounces white rum

1 ounce brandy

$1/_2$ ounce gin

1 ounce freshly squeezed orange juice

1 ounce freshly squeezed lemon juice

$1/_2$ ounce orgeat syrup

Place all ingredients in a cocktail shaker with cracked ice. Shake and strain into a Collins glass with ice cubes. Garnish with an orange wheel.

Hurricane

If you've ever been to the Big Easy, you've probably sipped this drink at Pat O'Brien's Bar in the French Quarter, where it was invented. Like the tropical storm for which it was named, the Hurricane is a stealth drink, deceptively calm at the outset but packing a wallop before you know it. For moderation's sake, we recommend sharing one with a friend.

$1 1/_2$ ounces light rum

$1 1/_2$ ounces dark rum

1 ounce freshly squeezed lime juice

1 ounce orange juice

2 ounces passion fruit juice

$1/_2$ tablespoon grenadine

Half fill a shaker with ice cubes, and add ingredients in the order given. Shake, then strain into a Collins or Hurricane glass filled with ice. Garnish with a slice of orange and a maraschino cherry.

Mai Tai

Without a doubt, the Mai Tai is the hands-down king of the tiki kingdom. Invented by Trader Vic Bergeron himself, it is a clever blend of sweet and pungent flavors. Although this cocktail dates back to the 1940s, chances are that the original recipe, given below, will be entirely new to you, since the trend of the past decades has been to make sweeter and sweeter Mai Tais using punchlike fruit juices. We urge you to go back to Bergeron's original for one simple reason — it's still the best we've tasted.

1 ounce light rum
1 ounce dark rum
1 1/2 ounces curaçao
1 1/2 teaspoons rock-candy syrup or simple syrup
1 1/2 teaspoons orgeat syrup

Place all ingredients in a cocktail shaker with cracked ice. Shake and strain into a chilled cocktail glass. Garnish with a strip of lime peel and a sprig of mint.

"There's been a lot of conversation over the beginning of the Mai Tai. And I want to get the record straight; I originated the Mai Tai. Many others have claimed credit. All this aggravates my ulcer completely. Anyone who says I didn't create this drink is a dirty stinker." — Vic Bergeron

Piña Colada

If the Mai Tai is the signature drink of Polynesian culture, the Piña Colada is the best known of the Caribbean cocktails. Its deceptively simple name is Spanish for "strained pineapple," yet the original Piña Colada was far from simple. Spanish-born Ricardo Garcia was the chief mixologist at the San Juan, Puerto Rico, Caribe Hilton Hotel in the 1950s and regularly mixed the house specialty for guests — a coconut-rum drink served in a freshly hollowed-out coconut. One day the local coconut cutters went on strike, leaving Garcia without "glasses" for his drink. Commandeering a supply of pineapples, he hollowed them out and used them instead. The flavor of pineapple went so well with the coconut, he began blending chunks of the fruit into the drink itself, then straining out the pineapple before serving so the drink retained its creamy texture. One of the Hilton corporation's most skilled and best-known bartenders, Garcia worked at many hotels within the chain, and his drink became a famous hit wherever he went.

Since the original recipe requires not only hollowing out a fresh pineapple but using a green coconut as well, we offer this easy-to-make updated version.

2 ounces light rum
$\frac{1}{2}$ ounce dark rum
2 ounces cream of coconut
2 to 3 ounces pineapple juice

Mix ingredients in a blender with a few scoops of crushed ice until smooth (about 10 seconds). Pour into a chilled Hurricane glass and garnish with a pineapple spear.
VARIATION: STRAWBERRY COLADA. Follow the recipe above, but add 1 ounce of fresh or frozen strawberries and one teaspoon of strawberry syrup or liqueur.

Bahama Mama

This drink combines a bouquet of tropical flavors — rum, coconut, pineapple, and citrus. The drink can easily become a confusion of competing flavors, as it does in recipes that add coffee liqueur as well, an innovation we do not recommend.

1 ounce rum
³/₄ ounce coconut rum
2 ounces orange juice
2 ounces pineapple juice
¹/₂ ounce lime juice
¹/₂ ounce grenadine

Place all ingredients in a shaker with cracked ice. Shake and strain into a chilled Collins glass. For garnish, thread an orange slice, pineapple chunk, and maraschino cherry onto a cocktail toothpick.

Planter's Punch

As with most punch recipes, there are many variations of this delightful cocktail. Key ingredients are rum and fruit juice, although some versions incorporate both rum and whiskey. The folks at Myer's Rum have long claimed credit for creating Planter's Punch, and we don't doubt them for a minute. Here is their recipe, which is as close to the "original" as you are likely to get.

1¹/₂ to 2 ounces Myer's dark rum
3 ounces orange juice
Juice of ¹/₂ lemon or lime
1 teaspoon superfine sugar
Dash of grenadine

Add ingredients, in order given, to a shaker, filled with cracked ice. Shake and strain into a chilled glass or a Collins glass filled with ice. Garnish with a slice of orange and a maraschino cherry.

VARIATION: In place of orange juice, use pineapple juice, and add a chunk of pineapple to the garnish.

47

Blue Lagoon

This cocktail was invented in the 1960s, when blue curaçao first appeared on the market. Its originator was Andy MacElhone, son of the legendary Harry of Harry's New York Bar in Paris.

1 1/2 ounces vodka
1/2 ounce blue curaçao
Freshly squeezed lemon juice

Pour vodka and curaçao into a glass with several ice cubes. Top with lemon juice. Stir, then garnish with a slice of lemon and a maraschino cherry.

VARIATION: Replace lemon juice with pineapple juice; garnish with a slice of pineapple.
VARIATION: BLUE SHARK. Replace lemon juice with 1 ounce of tequila. Combine all ingredients in a shaker with cracked ice. Shake and strain into a chilled cocktail glass.

Blue Hawaii

Every January 8, when the winds are whipping up snow squalls and the skies are low and gray, we break out the blue curaçao, make one of these, and put on some Elvis music. What better way to celebrate the birthday of the king of rock and roll?

1 ounce blue curaçao
1/2 ounce dark rum
1/2 ounce light rum
1 ounce orange juice
5 ounces pineapple juice

Combine ingredients in a shaker with ice. Shake, then strain into a tall, ice-filled glass. Garnish with an orange slice, a pineapple chunk, and a maraschino cherry.

VARIATION: FROZEN BLUE HAWAII. Reduce pineapple juice to three ounces. Place ingredients in a blender with 3 to 4 ounces of ice. Blend; omit garnish.
VARIATION: Replace orange juice with 1/2 ounce crème de banane.

Sloe Gin Sling

The Singapore Sling — which did indeed originate in Singapore — dates back to the 1930s. Trader Vic's version, made with sloe gin, was a popular update in the 1960s.

³/₄ ounce gin
³/₄ ounce sloe gin
1¹/₂ ounces cherry brandy
1 ounce Benedictine
Juice from half a lime
Club soda

Combine all ingredients except club soda in a mixing glass with ice cubes. Stir, then strain into a Collins glass with ice. Fill to top with club soda and garnish with a twist of lime peel.

VARIATION: Ginger ale in place of club soda is particularly popular in the Pacific.

VARIATION: ORIGINAL SINGAPORE SLING. To make the original, drier version of this drink, eliminate the sloe gin and increase the amount of regular gin to 1¹/₂ ounces.

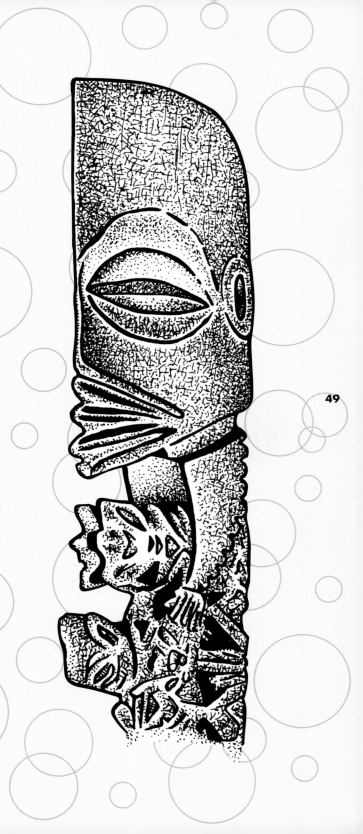

Foliage and Frosted Glass: The Fern Bar Era

For young unmarrieds, the 1960s seemed to have it all. Great music. The Pill. Cheap apartments. One little problem, though. Once that B.A. degree had been converted into the seedling of a career, where did nice girls go to meet nice boys? No sooner had the 1960s drawn to a close than dating problems became a favorite theme, reflected in books, movies, and TV sitcoms — just ask Mary Richards, the Minneapolis career girl played by Mary Tyler Moore, who suffered through two dozen boyfriends in seven seasons and never did find Mr. Right.

"I know exactly where I was twelve years ago.
I was at a party like this, sitting on a couch like this, drinking wine from
a paper cup like this. You've come a long way, baby."
Rhoda Morgenstern (Valerie Harper), The Mary Tyler Moore Show

In real life, of course, boys and girls did manage to get together. And appearing on the scene to help them do so was a phenomenon known as the fern bar. Much maligned today as dens of overly sweet drinks, Barry Manilow music, and not nearly enough iniquity, the fern bar was once an important innovation, and we'd like to put in a good word for it. It was the fern bar, after all, that brought us such indispensable artifacts as faux Tiffany lamps, silk foliage, and broccoli quiche — and who would really want to live without those?

The establishment widely credited with being the first fern bar was Henry Africa's, which opened in San Francisco in 1970. Africa, whose real name was Norman Hobday, realized that to bring single women as well as single men into a drinking establishment, the establishment had to be redesigned from the ground up. Africa abolished the grimly plain, masculine-style bar of previous generations and created a bar with a furnished environment and plenty of distractions. Mixing themes with abandon, Africa loaded his bar with upholstered couches, stained-glass lamps, lush ferns, and big-game trophies. He threw in some model trains for good measure, a conversation piece that gave perfect strangers something to talk about until they got past the first awkward moments.

While we don't want to take anything away from Henry Africa, we feel not enough credit has been given to an equally innovative East Coast operation. In 1965, T.G.I. Friday's

opened on Manhattan's Upper East Side. Like Henry Africa's, T.G.I. Friday's featured a well-appointed atmosphere calculated to make female patrons feel at ease. The establishment's red-and-white striped awnings and tablecloths, brass rails, bentwood chairs, and Tiffany-esque light fixtures suggested a gilded age of innocent fun. But the biggest innovation was artfully blending casual dining into the mix. Young professionals who might be embarrassed to hang out in a bar hoping to meet someone had no problem dining out with friends. Soon police barricades had to be erected to help manage the crowds waiting to get in, and *Newsweek* magazine identified T.G.I. Friday's as *the* meeting spot for singles. Within a few years, the strip of First Avenue it anchored became a mile-long playground of clubs, bars, and restaurants catering to upscale unmarrieds.

By the mid-1970s, almost every town in America had at least one fern bar. The look — polished brass, dark wood, leaded-glass windows, and lots of foliage — was widely copied. Ditto the food-to-eat-while-flirting menu. Who can remember the 1970s without remembering baked potato skins, stuffed mushrooms, quiche, and Buffalo wings (which, appropriately enough, were invented at the Anchor Bar in Buffalo, New York)? At some point, the much-copied atmosphere became a cliché, and the fern bar lost its appeal. Henry Africa's closed its doors in 1987, the manager noting that "The fern bar is a formula now." Or maybe it had just fulfilled its purpose, allowing a whole generation of singles ot meet up, pair off, and fade into a suburban welter of strollers, mortgages, and BABY ON BOARD signs. At any rate, the fern bar faded fast, and today few former patrons will even admit to having set foot inside one.

FERN BAR DRINKS

Fern bars, with their gussied-up interiors and bland music, soon became easy targets for derision, especially derision from men. The world was getting just a little bit too frilly, and fern bars were part of the problem. Books like *Real Men Don't Eat Quiche* (1982) and the return of ruggedly male characters like TV's J.R. Ewing of *Dallas* (beginning in 1979) marked a beachhead of rebellion.

"The tough guy finds himself besieged with female admirers, while the self-effacing friend sadly clutches his glass of Chablis at the fern bar alone."
— Demonic Males, Richard Wrangham & Dale Peterson

For proof positive that fern bars were part of the problem, one needed to look no farther than a drink menu. In place of strong and bracing cocktails, a host of sweet mixed drinks had sprung up, many of them named after favorite confections. This class of drinks became known as "girl drinks," — but that didn't squelch their popularity or deter "real men" from ordering them. We offer their recipes in the spirit of nostalgia, but even we, adventurous mixologists that we are, wonder at their popularity, for they are the kind of sweet mixtures that produce the worst of hangovers.

Fuzzy Navel

A classic fern bar drink, whose whimsical name is not nearly as mysterious as one might imagine. It simply represents the two fruit flavors involved — "fuzzy" peaches and "navel" oranges.

1 1/2 ounces peach schnapps
Chilled orange juice

Place several ice cubes in a Highball glass. Pour schnapps over the ice, then fill the glass with orange juice.

VARIATION: FIREFLY. Place several ice cubes in a Highball glass. Pour 1 ounce of schnapps and 1 ounce of vodka over the ice, then fill the glass with orange juice. We have often seen this recipe referred to as a Fuzzy Navel. Whichever name it goes by, it is less sweet than the original Fuzzy Navel, above.

VARIATION: FUZZY FRUIT. Another version designed to cut the sweetness. To make this drink, follow the directions for a Fuzzy Navel, but use grapefruit juice in place of orange juice.

Tootsie Roll

For those who can't decide whether candy is dandy or liquor is quicker, this drink offers both. Wildly popular throughout the 1970s, it's a blast of pure nostalgia.

1½ ounces dark crème de cacao
Chilled orange juice

Fill a Highball glass with ice. Pour in crème de cacao, then fill with orange juice. Many recipes call for coffee liqueur instead of crème de cacao, an equally legitimate version of the drink. We remember both being made during the 1970s.

VARIATION: Elaborate, carefully mixed drinks were definitely not the signature of most fern bars, but if they had been, this version of the Tootsie Roll might have supplanted the original. Pour 1½ ounces dark crème de cacao over ice in a cocktail shaker. Add a splash of orange juice and a splash of cream or half and half. Shake, then strain into a chilled cocktail glass.

Lemon Drop

The key to this fern bar favorite is to serve it ice-cold. A lukewarm Lemon Drop has no appeal whatsoever. For best results, it should be served in a well-chilled glass.

1½ ounces plain or lemon vodka
¾ ounce chilled fresh lemon juice
1 teaspoon sugar

Pour vodka and lemon juice over cracked ice in a cocktail shaker. Add sugar and shake well to ensure that the sugar is dissolved. Strain into a chilled cocktail glass and garnish with a slice of lemon.

Creamsicle

As far as we have been able to ascertain, the Creamsicle began as an alcohol-free drink, a combination of orange juice and cream or ice cream. Hence, there are many alcoholic versions of this cocktail, incorporating everything from amaretto to Kahlúa to Grand Marnier. The version below is one of the best we've sampled.

1/2 ounce vodka
1/2 ounce triple sec
1 ounce chilled orange juice
1 ounce cream or half-and-half

Pour all ingredients into a cocktail shaker partly filled with ice. Shake and strain into a cocktail glass.

Del Monte Cocktail

This fruit cocktail of a drink is actually a variation of the much older — and now almost forgotten — Clover Club cocktail. It owes its existence to the tiki craze, which popularized rum as a viable spirit for cocktails.

1 1/2 ounces light rum
3/4 ounce fresh lemon juice
Splash of grenadine

Pour rum over cracked ice in a cocktail shaker. Add lemon juice and grenadine, shake, and strain into a cocktail glass. As with most drinks involving citrus juices, this one is only good if it is served cold, so remember to chill your glass beforehand.

VARIATION: CLOVER CLUB. The great-great-grandmother of the Del Monte, the Clover Club dates back to the days when gin cocktails were the "it" drinks of the moment. To prepare, follow the directions for the Del Monte, above, but use 1 1/2 ounces of gin in place of rum. The original Clover Club also included a raw egg white, which — times, tastes, and health regulations being what they are — we generally omit.

Cosmopolitan

Credit for the invention of this drink most often goes to the bartenders of Provincetown, Rhode Island. Whatever its origins, its popularity spread up and down the eastern seaboard, then jumped to the West Coast to become the toast of San Francisco. Wildly popular in singles bars of the 1970s, it was a refreshingly tart alternative to the generally sweet fern bar drinks of the era.

1 1/2 ounces vodka
1 1/2 ounces cranberry juice
1/2 ounce Cointreau
1/2 ounce freshly squeezed lime juice

Place ingredients in a cocktail shaker with cracked ice. Shake briskly and strain into a chilled cocktail glass. Garnish with a twist of lime.

Mirror Ball

"The best discotheque DJs are underground stars,
discovering previously ignored albums, foreign imports, album cuts, and
obscure singles with the power to make the crowd scream and playing them
overlapped, nonstop so you dance until you drop."
— The first published article on disco: "Discotheque Rock '72: Paaaaarty!"
by Vince Aletti, Rolling Stone, September 13, 1973

It gave us swirling skirts and stiletto heels, tight white pants, fussy shirts, and coiffed hair. It made supernova celebrities of Liza and Halston and jolted Travolta's career. The music wasn't great — unless, of course, you wanted to dance, and then it was terrific.

Disco, the big entertainment of the 1970s, had its origins in occupied France. When German troops took control of Paris, they closed down the city's flourishing jazz clubs. Music enthusiasts were forced underground, to gather in clandestine cellar cabarets where they listened, with secret joy, to recorded music. One of the clubs dubbed itself La Discothèque, and the name became generic for any club playing recorded music. Instead of disappearing after the war, the clubs flourished. Paul Racine opened Whiskey a Go-Go, while one of his protégés, Regina Zyberberg, opened the famous Chez Régine. Dancing to recorded music was suddenly chic. If Brigitte Bardot and Georges Pompidou found it amusing, shouldn't everyone?

Discotheques could soon be found in capitals throughout Europe, catering to a relatively well-heeled clientele of upper-class youth, celebrities, and wandering Americans. In New

York, Le Club opened its doors and enjoyed a heady reign as the place to be until it was displaced by the Peppermint Lounge in the early 1960s.

At the same time, another style of disco was inventing itself — a rougher, rowdier style born in America's urban funk clubs. Long before *Saturday Night Fever* arrived at a theater near you, funk-born disco was working its way up the social ladder and into the mainstream. Like the original clubs of WWII Paris, the first American clubs flourished in cellars, lofts, and abandoned warehouses. Inevitably, however, American funk collided with Euro-style disco. The result was a confetti swirl of noise and glitter that became Disco with a capital D. Clubs competed with each other to be bigger and flashier, to have a more kaleidoscopic display of lights and a higher-volume sound system. DJs, the *chefs de cuisine* of the nightly fare, became well-known celebrities, lured from club to club by ever-increasing salaries. Step by step, disco became theater. Regine introduced the idea of staging "happenings" (one of the most memorable of which was platinum-blonde night), and clubs from Woonsocket to Walnut Creek followed suit.

In this delirious and dizzy state, disco existed exuberantly for nearly a decade. Though some decry it as an all-too-typical offering of the culturally lost 1970s, they forget there was a time when hopping around to "YMCA" actually seemed fresh and even mildly iconoclastic. Disco clubs were the first cultural phenomenon where the vision of a rainbowed America actually existed. Prior to the disco era, and often since, clubs divided along predictable lines — black clubs, white clubs, gay clubs, straight clubs, celebrity hangouts, and urban dives. Everyone danced together at disco clubs, not

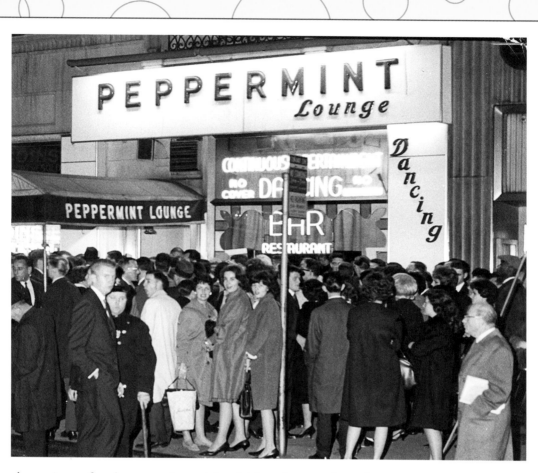

always in perfect harmony but with a higher degree of social integration than had been seen before.

After a happy decade, disco died a mercifully quick death. Between 1981 and 1982, it all but vanished from the scene. The twin streams of music feeding the hopper — black funk and white rock — had been melded into a colorless, corporatized genre despairingly referred to as "beige" music. Serious musicians sought other outlets for their talent, giving birth to the New Wave trend that would dominate the 1980s. Clubs ran into trouble as well, some with tax problems, some with DJs who spent more time in the bathroom with a rolled-up dollar bill or a small silver spoon than they did in the DJ's booth. One of disco's key ingredients — teeming crowds who'd stand in a rope line in the pouring rain — ran on to the next party. The glitter was gone, and by 1983 disco seemed as quaint and outmoded as the tea dances of the roaring 1920s.

THE CLUB

It may not have been the biggest, the best, or the most innovative, but almost from the moment it opened, Studio 54 was the best-known disco club of all time, its name known the world over, its guest list of regulars — Warhol, Halston, Diana Ross, Liza Minnelli, Bianca Jagger — a veritable who's-who of late-1970s stardom. Even Salvador Dali was seen there.

Located on Manhattan's West 54th Street, the space was football-field huge, theatrical, and haunted by a glittering array of Broadway ghosts. It had housed an opera company in the 1920s, a host of theaters and the Casino de Paris nightclub in the 1930s, and in the 1940s and 1950s, the CBS studio from which *Beat the Clock, The $64,000 Question,* and *The Johnny Carson Show* were beamed, live from coast-to-coast. (It was this final use that inspired the club's name.) The balcony and stage area, still structurally intact, were left in place and given a dazzling refurbish. A mirrored bar was positioned under the balcony, and just beyond it spread the huge dance floor, lit by columns of strobe lights that hung from the ceiling like pulsing stalactites. Silver banquettes and a scattering of tables ringed the floor — comfortable seating from which to observe what was surely the gaudiest show in town. The most coveted regions of the club were off-limits to most patrons — the side door reserved for

celebrity entrances and exits and a private lounge downstairs where only a cluster of hand-picked VIPs were allowed.

On any given night — including opening night, when even invited guests were turned away — the crowds were large and the competition to get in fierce. Contrary to popular myth, it wasn't necessarily youth, beauty, or wealth that got you in. Owners Steve Rubell and Ian Schrager realized early on that disco was live theater, and more than anything they wanted a good cast for the show. Their directions to the doormen were to "mix a perfect salad" each night, and if you were a tomato on a night they needed more lettuce, too bad. On a snowy New Year's Eve in 1977, Nile Rodgers and Bernard Edwards of Chic were invited to the club by Grace Jones, who was performing there. Despite their credentials, they failed to get in. Annoyed, the boys went home and wrote a revenge song, whose refrain was "Fuck off." Realizing that the song had merit, they cleaned up the no-airplay lyric and got their revenge — issued as "Le Freak," it topped the charts for six straight weeks and was played at virtually every disco in the world.

With the doormen mixing the perfect salad, even an ordinary night at Studio 54 could be pretty spectacular. But the extraordinary nights hit heights not seen in New York

Dance to the Music

A dozen great songs of the era. Enjoy them with a long, tall cocktail. We dare you not to hum along.

"Copacabana," Barry Manilow

"Heart of Glass," Blondie

"The Hustle," Van McCoy

"I Will Survive," Gloria Gaynor

"Last Dance," Donna Summer

"Le Freak," Chic

"Shake Your Booty," KC & the Sunshine Band

"Stayin' Alive," Bee Gees

"Turn the Beat Around," Vickie Sue Robinson

"Upside Down," Diana Ross

"We Are Family," Sister Sledge

"YMCA," Village People

since the Four Hundred held butterfly balls and horseback banquets. At the Bianca Jagger birthday party, held in May 1977, the guest of honor arrived on a white horse, led in by a strapping young man clad only in body paint.

So large does Studio 54 loom in the collective consciousness that few realize how short-lived the club was. It opened on April 26, 1977, and closed in March of 1980, just a little more than a month after owners Rubell and Schrager began serving jail time for income-tax evasion and slightly after the club's liquor license expired — a death blow to any club. (Rumor has it that 54's last legal drink was enjoyed by Sylvester Stallone.)

The club was sold to Mark Fleischman and reopened in September 1981 with the former owners — now out of jail — acting as consultants. The world had moved on, though, and Studio 54 never regained its former glitter. It closed for good in 1986.

DISCO DRINKS

Dancing was thirsty business, and drinks that typify the disco era are invariably tall and wet. No egg-cup–sized cocktails here. If you're having a disco party, we recommend laying in a supply of tall Collins glasses and stocking up on mixers, as guests will invariably drink more than they ordinarily would.

Melonball

Everybody wanted to be at Studio 54, even liqueurs of foreign extraction. In 1978, when Japan-based Suntory decided to launch its popular melon liqueur, Midori, in America, it chose Studio 54 as the site. The party was attended by stars from *Saturday Night Fever*, while the movie's closing credits rolled over an image of the Midori billboard in Times Square. Midori became a huge hit, and Midori-based cocktails are an enduring legacy of the disco era. The Melonball is one of the most popular.

2 ounces melon liqueur
1 ounce vodka
4 ounces of either
pineapple or grapefruit
juice (your choice)

Half-fill a Collins glass with ice cubes. Pour liqueur and vodka over the ice, then fill the glass with fruit juice. As with any drink requiring fruit juice, this one will taste best with fresh juice or, at the very least, juice that is not from a concentrate.

Stoned Sunrise

Mick Jagger and his then-wife, Bianca, were among the celebrities frequently spotted at New York's Studio 54, which makes it all the more fitting that we offer here the Rolling Stones' own invigorating — if slightly stupefying — version of the Tequila Sunrise. According to Jill Spalding, the author of *Blythe Spirits*, Mick and the boys referred to it simply as the "In Drink." In what, or whom, we cannot be certain.

3 ounces tequila
3 ounces orange juice
3/4 ounce grenadine

Mix tequila and orange juice in a shaker with cracked ice. Pour ice and all into a Collins glass, adding additional ice if needed. Slowly pour in grenadine, but do not stir. Garnish with a slice of lime.

VARIATION: For a slightly drier drink, add the juice of half a lime to the orange juice and tequila before shaking.

TRADITIONAL TEQUILA SUNRISE: To make this classic, simply reduce the amount of tequila to 1 1/2 ounces and mix as described above.

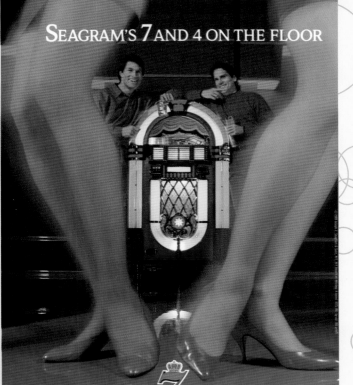

SEAGRAM'S 7 AND 4 ON THE FLOOR

Wine Cooler

As standard as Perrier throughout the 1970s, the Wine Cooler was the perfect disco drink, refreshingly thirst-quenching and mild enough to keep you relatively sober. Today, the drink has become a well-known staple, as comforting and familiar as an old friend. And like old friends, this one sometimes gets taken for granted. The fact is, few people know how to make this simple drink properly. Americans, especially, are prone to adulterating it with all sorts of additives, including lemonade. A few minutes of thoughtful study will break you of these inclinations and give you a whole new perspective on this timeless classic.

ORIGINAL WINE COOLER

We begin our quest for the perfect Cooler in the land where it all began, Austria. There, the drink is known as a Wine Spritzer, and is made strictly according to the recipe below

**Soda water, preferably from an
   old-fashioned bottle**
**Dry, acidic white wine that has been
   thoroughly chilled**

Fill a glass slightly more than $1/8$ full with soda water. Top with chilled wine and enjoy.

"Disgusting practices like drinking with ice or perverting the drink with a slice of lemon are to be considered completely inadmissable!"
— Best-of-Austria Web site

CLASSIC AMERICAN WINE COOLER

Because the only drink Americans can endure without ice is cocoa, we hasten to offer the drink's classic American version as well:

White wine of choice
Club soda or lemon-lime soda

Fill a tall glass with ice cubes. Fill $3/4$ full with wine, then top with soda.

WINE COOLER VARIATIONS

Once you understand the basic concept, the Wine Cooler offers itself up for myriad variations, some of them surprisingly delicious. So — with many apologies to our Austrian friends — we suggest you branch out and try some of these:

- **DISCO SALLY:** White wine and tonic.
- **CHERRY COOLER:** Cherry wine and cola.
- **PEACH COOLER:** Peach wine and lemon-lime soda.
- **RHUBARB COOLER:** Rhubarb wine and club soda. (If you have rhubarb growing in your yard, cut a few ruby stalks to use as swizzle sticks.)
- **APPLE-CRANBERRY COOLER:** Apple wine and cranberry juice.
- **STRAWBERRY COOLER:** Strawberry wine and orange juice.

Caffeine Mania

The steamed, creamed, cinnamoned, and spiced lattés of today would make a true coffee maven blush. Coffee gained its toehold as an inexpensive, no-nonsense drink valued for its stimulative powers. Colonists and pioneers, cowboys, and Swedish lumberjacks all favored coffee for its stimulating effects, and Melissa Clark's *The Coffee Book* has gone so far as to link the spread of coffee's popularity to the rise of the Protestant work ethic. One of the oddest episodes in coffee's edgy history has to be an ad campaign of the late 1970s. Celebrating a buzzed-up generation of "Coffee Achievers," the campaign positioned coffee as a sort of legal amphetamine, a substance that unleashed big dreams and the manic energy surges needed to make them come true. Whether or not this campaign led to the coffee culture that followed is uncertain — but from there it was only a hop, skip, and jump to coffee's use as a cocktail mixer.

68

Mudslide

There are numerous versions of the Mudslide, and not all of them have coffee. This one does and is one of the nicest we've tasted.

1 ounce vodka
1 ounce Irish cream liqueur
1 ounce coffee liqueur
6–8 ounces hot coffee
1 scoop of vanilla ice cream

Place vodka, liqueurs, and coffee together in a metal tumbler or tempered glass. Add the ice cream, stir, and serve immediately.

Irish Coffee

Though workingmen had probably been adding whiskey to their coffee for years, it wasn't until the postwar years that that the drink became official. A barman at Ireland's Shannon Airport, looking for a comforting drink to appeal to his American customers, reinvented the traditional Irish drink of whiskey and tea. He replaced the tea with coffee, added sugar, and topped the hot drink off with a dollop of whipped Irish cream. The drink was first served in America at the Buena Vista at San Francisco's Fisherman's Wharf and by the 1960s and 1970s was a popular staple throughout the country.

1 1/2 ounces Irish whiskey
2 teaspoons light brown sugar
4 ounces hot coffee
Lightly whipped cream

Place whiskey and sugar in a coffee cup and stir to dissolve sugar. Add hot coffee. Top with a generous dollop of whipped cream. Make sure to add the whipped cream gently, floating it on the coffee rather than letting it sink in. Freshly whipped cream is best, but if you are using aerosol cream, express it onto a spoon first, then transfer gently to the coffee. If desired, sprinkle lightly with cinnamon.

VARIATION: AMARETTO COFFEE. Replace Irish whiskey with Amaretto.

VARIATION: JAMAICAN COFFEE. Replace Irish whiskey with 1/2 ounce each of cognac, coffee liqueur, and dark rum. Sprinkle whipped cream with a pinch of ground ginger.

VARIATION: MEXICAN COFFEE. Use a coffee liqueur, such as Kahlúa or Tia Maria, in place of Irish whiskey.

VARIATION: CAFÉ ROYALE. Use cognac instead of Irish whiskey and 1 teaspoon of white sugar instead of brown.

VARIATION: CANADIAN COFFEE. Use Canadian whiskey instead of Irish whiskey and 2 to 3 teaspoons of maple syrup instead of sugar.

VARIATION: COFFEE NUDGE. Replace Irish whiskey with 1/2 ounce each of brandy, coffee liqueur, and dark crème de cacao. Sprinkle whipped cream with grated chocolate or cocoa powder.

VARIATION: ITALIAN COFFEE. Use sambuca instead of Irish whiskey and top whipped cream with a coffee bean.

The Sexually Liberated Cocktail

I t all started in the libertine 1920s, when formerly polite cocktail menus began acquiring drinks with names like Between the Sheets and the Angel's Tit. Alas, the slightly naughty cocktail vanished with Prohibition and remained in hiding during the buttoned-down postwar years. But you can keep a winning idea down only so long, and in the 1960s sex — and sexy cocktails — made a *big* comeback in America.

THE 1960s — THE MAKING OF A SEXUAL REVOLUTION

1960

- Birth-control pills become available in the United States.
- Carefree, curvaceous Barbie becomes the most popular doll in America after just one year on the shelves. Besides her glamorous wardrobe, Barbie will eventually acquire a boyfriend, a dream house, a sports car, and numerous other status symbols.

1961

- *Divorce Italian Style* hits the movie theaters and introduces Americans to the possibilities of the continental lifestyle.
- Henry Miller's long-banned novel, *The Tropic of Cancer,* is released in the U.S. for the first time.

1962

- For those who haven't read the book, Stanley Kubrick's film version of *Lolita* gives middle-aged men plenty to think about.
- *Sex and the Single Girl*, by Helen Gurley Brown, tops the bestseller charts by promising that "any girl, even a poor or plain one, can have a rich, full life of dating."

1963

- Betty Friedan's book *The Feminine Mystique* tells women it's OK to put down the pots and pans.
- More than fifty girls per week apply to *Playboy* magazine in hopes of becoming a Miss January, or any of the eleven other delectable months.

"The only question I ever ask any woman is, 'What time is your husband coming home?'"
— Paul Newman in Hud, 1963

1964

- *Candy*, about a promiscuous but innocent coed, is published in the U.S. after more than six years of nonstop popularity in France. Authors Terry Southern and Mason Hoffenberg single-handedly boost interest in college enrollment.
- Discos feature go-go girls dancing on raised platforms. One San Francisco nightspot introduces topless dancers in the summer. By September, the girls are bottomless as well.

1965

- The Rolling Stones' "Satisfaction" is a worldwide hit. Though Mick Jagger's diction is often hard to understand, his point is more than clear.
- Body painting is the new fad. It isn't long until edible paint comes on the market as well.

1966

- *The Human Sexual Response* by Masters and Johnson keeps America up nights — reading.
- Raquel Welch wears a fur bikini in *One Million Years B.C.* According to the poster, the movie depicts "a savage world whose only law was lust."

STUDENTS SEDUCED THE TEACHERS IN THIS —

LUST SCHOOL

75¢
NB 1654

BY TONY CALVANO

THIS IS AN ORIGINAL NIGHTSTAND BOOK

1967

- The first "Be-in" is held in Golden Gate Park in San Francisco, attracting huge numbers of young people and setting the stage for a whole lot of horsing around.
- Everybody buys Desmond Morris's *The Naked Ape* for the sex parts, making it an instant bestseller.

1968

- The world's "first tribal-love-rock musical" — *Hair* — opens off-off-Broadway. Nudity becomes an option for costume designers everywhere.
- In the movie *Barbarella,* Jane Fonda fends off a fatal, machine-driven orgasm by turning the tables on the machine and shorting it out.

1969

- *Naked Came the Stranger,* by the pseudonymous Penelope Ash, tops bestseller lists and causes nationwide buzz. Eventually, the anatomically knowledgeable Ms. Ash is revealed to be a group of staff writers from *New York Newsday.*
- The film *I Am Curious Yellow* triggers a wave of highbrow skin flicks, allowing moviegoers to feel like intelligentsia rather than voyeurs.
- Half a million Baby Boomers flock to the Woodstock Music & Art Fair, and 1969 becomes forever known as "the summer of love." Some say it was all downhill from there.

WHAT TO DRINK DURING A SEXUAL REVOLUTION

With so much teasing sensuality in the air, it was only a matter of time until libations followed libido. Once again, saucily named cocktails became the vogue. Here are a few favorites.

Like sex itself, these recipes — and many others of the era — are very much a matter of personal taste, with many variations. We offer our favorites here but would never go so far as to claim that our position is the only one.

DIVINE SCREWS

Why settle for an ordinary screw when you can have one that is slow or comfortable or — better yet — slow *and* comfortable? We're talking Screw*drivers*, of course, and shame on you for thinking anything else.

Classic Slow Screw

The original Screwdriver was a man's drink, one that got its name when an engineer used his screwdriver as a swizzle stick to mix his vodka and orange juice. But in the 1960s, so-called girl drinks began to supplant more masculine libations like Martinis and — yes — Screwdrivers. The Slow Screw came into its own, boosted to popularity by its vibrant beauty. The drink's key ingredient is sloe gin, which isn't a true gin at all but a liqueur made by adding sugar and sloes (the plumlike berries of the blackthorn bush) to gin. As the liqueur ages, it turns a rich shade of red. The classic Slow Screw is an unquestionably sweet drink, typical of the era when the Pill, hot pants, and bra burnings were just coming into fashion.

1 1/2 ounces sloe gin
Orange juice

To make a Slow Screw, place ice cubes in an Old Fashioned glass, pour the sloe gin over the ice, then fill with orange juice. By tradition, this drink is not garnished.

VARIATION: SALTY DOG. This is one of the most popular of all variations on the Screwdriver. To make it, combine 1 1/2 ounces of regular gin with grapefruit juice.

VARIATION: CONTEMPORARY SLOW SCREW. America's taste for sweet drinks has waned, so this contemporary version uses only 1/2 ounce sloe gin and adds 1 ounce of vodka.

Comfortable Screw

Southern Comfort had been around since 1894, but it got a big boost in the 1960s when rock star Janis Joplin popularized it as her beverage of choice. Joplin's wonderfully raspy voice made cigarettes and whiskey seem like a good thing indeed, and Comfortable Screws became a standard in the competent bartender's repertoire.

1 ounce Southern Comfort
1 ounce vodka
Orange juice

Place ice cubes in a Collins glass, pour the Southern Comfort and vodka over the ice, then fill with orange juice and stir well.

Slow Comfortable Screw

Once Slow Screws and Comfortable Screws were introduced, drinkers and bartenders just couldn't help playing along. As a result, there are dozens of drinks with these slightly naughty names. Many — including one we sampled called a "Slow Screw Against the Wall in the Dark Side of Mexico City" — are more fun to ask for than to actually drink. A notable exception is the Sloe Comfortable Screw, which has now become a contemporary classic.

³/₄ ounce sloe gin
³/₄ ounce vodka
³/₄ ounce Southern Comfort
Orange Juice

Place ice cubes in a Collins glass, pour sloe gin, Southern Comfort, and vodka over the ice, then fill with orange juice and stir. Garnish with a slice of orange.

OH, THOSE ORGASMS

What's the difference between an Orgasm and a Screaming Orgasm? A Screaming Orgasm and a Multiple Orgasm? You probably have to be there to know for certain, and we found bartenders' recipes for these as interchangeable as Elizabeth Taylor's husbands. Our advice: If you don't enjoy your first time — try it again.

Orgasm

³/₄ ounce Irish cream liqueur
³/₄ ounce coffee liqueur
³/₄ ounce almond liqueur

Combine in a cocktail shaker with cracked ice. Shake and strain into a chilled cocktail glass.

VARIATION: If you don't have almond liqueur on hand, you can have a perfectly legitimate Orgasm by mixing 1¹/₂ ounces each of coffee and Irish cream liqueurs.

Screaming Orgasm

³/₄ ounce vodka
³/₄ ounce Irish cream liqueur
³/₄ ounce coffee liqueur
³/₄ ounce almond liqueur

Combine in a cocktail shaker with cracked ice. Shake and strain into a chilled cocktail glass.

Multiple Orgasm

¹/₂ ounce vodka
¹/₂ ounce Irish cream liqueur
¹/₂ ounce coffee liqueur
¹/₂ ounce almond liqueur
2 ounces light cream or half-and-half

Combine in a cocktail shaker with cracked ice. Shake gently and strain into a chilled Highball glass.

Pink Pussycat

Long before men were from Mars and women were from Venus, the French had it all figured out: Women were felines, men were canines. If you doubt the logic of this equation, take another look at Elizabeth Taylor as Maggie ("the Cat") in Tennessee Williams's *Cat on a Hot Tin Roof* or Honor Blackman as Pussy Galore in *Goldfinger*. It goes without saying that wherever titilating innuendo goes, a cocktail of one sort or another soon follows. Hence, the Pink Pussycat.

1½ ounces vodka
Pineapple juice
Grenadine

James Bond (Sean Connery): Who are you?
Pussy Galore (Honor Blackman): My name is Pussy Galore.
Bond: I must be dreaming.
— *Goldfinger* (1964)

Place ice in a Highball glass, add vodka, and fill with pineapple juice. Top with a splash of grenadine.

VARIATION: Many versions of this libation use grapefruit juice rather than pineapple. We prefer pineapple, but, as with the dance between the sexes, to each his own.

Slippery Nipple

The standard components of a Slippery Nipple are equal parts sambuca and Irish cream liqueur. The drink is prepared in a shot glass by pouring the sambuca in first and then gently floating the Irish cream liqueur on top, so that two distinct layers form. Many mixologists add a suggestive dot of grenadine on top, but we feel that is a case of gilding the, er, lily.

VARIATION: If a Slippery Nipple doesn't pacify your craving, why not try a Buttery Nipple? To make this delight, follow the directions for a Slippery Nipple, but use butterscotch schnapps in place of sambuca.

Silk Panties

What goes down smoother than Silk Panties? This libation is similar to Sex on the Beach but is cut down to the bare essentials.

1 ounce vodka
1 ounce peach schnapps

Combine one ounce each of vodka and peach schnapps in a cocktail shaker with cracked ice. Shake, then strain into a cocktail glass with ice.

VARIATION: To make this drink shot-style, use $1/2$ ounce each of vodka and schnapps, mix with ice, and strain into a shot glass.

VARIATION: ITALIAN SILK PANTIES. To go continental, use sambuca in place of the vodka.

Sex on the Beach

Much nicer than real sex on the beach — far more thirst-quenching, and so much less sand to deal with!

1 ounce vodka
1 ounce peach schnapps
2 to 3 ounces orange juice
2 to 3 ounces cranberry juice

Fill a Collins glass with ice cubes. Add vodka and schnapps. Fill glass to the top with equal parts orange and cranberry juice, then stir. Garnish with a wedge of lime.

VARIATION: We've seen this popular version referred to as Sex on Miami Beach, but just as many sippers refer to it simply as Sex on the Beach. To make this tropical-tasting version, replace the peach schnapps with melon liqueur and use pineapple juice in place of orange juice.

VARIATION: To make a Sex on the Beach shot, use equal parts of each ingredient, combine in a cocktail shaker with crushed ice, shake, and strain into a glass.

Toga! Drinks for the Degree-Challenged

A quick glance at classic college libations is a good argument for raising the legal drinking age to 25 or even 30. Fortunately, more people claim to have spent their college days in a daze than ever considered doing so. In fact, about the only people who don't brag about drinking too much in college are Baby Boomers, who brag instead about the drugs they did. But here, for purposes of nostalgia, are the drinks that first caught your eye when you were young, broke, and absolutely desperate for a good time.

Hop Skip and Go Naked

Hop Skip and Go Naked is a recent version of an evil concoction that, we suspect, has long been part of the college scene — the pour-it-all-in punch, as in "Kegger at 410 Maple Street! Bring whatever!" We didn't hear the title Hop Skip and Go Naked until sometime in the 1980s but can vouch for the fact that a similar kind of party punch went by the name Hairy Buffalo at the University of Indiana in the 1960s — a name used by bartenders to denote a blend mixed from leftover or mixed-by-mistake cocktails.

Refined instructions call for Hop Skip and Go Naked punch to be mixed in pitchers or coolers, but we have also seen recipes instructing party-givers to double or triple the recipe and "Mix ingredients in a garbage can, preferably a new one." Recipes tend to be free-form when they are followed at all, but this one provides some basic guidelines.

Fifth of vodka
6-pack of beer
3 cans of frozen lemon-lime drink concentrate

Mix together with lots of ice, stirring to bring up a froth. Drink from plastic cups.

Wapatula

We haven't discovered the origin of the name, but Wapatula parties (or Wapatulies, as they were sometimes called) were popular on Minnesota campuses at the end of the 1960s. In the recipe below, one can see the tropical refinements of the tiki influence.

1 gallon vodka
1 bottle Tom Collins mix
Fruit punch to taste
2 large cans diced pineapple, with juice
1 sliced lime
Sugar to taste

Mix with ice in a cooler or vat and drink up. Headache guaranteed.

Bay Breeze

A variation of the much older Sea Breeze, the Bay Breeze is a campus favorite for the same reason the earlier drink was — it's a stealth cocktail that lowers inhibitions quickly, with little or no warning.

1 ½ ounces vodka
Pineapple juice
Cranberry juice

Place a generous amount of ice in a Highball glass. Pour vodka over the ice, fill glass with ²/₃ pineapple juice to ¹/₃ cranberry juice.

VARIATION: MADRAS. Named for its vibrant colors, this Highball is definitely part of the Breeze family. Follow the instructions above, but replace the cranberry juice with orange juice.

VARIATION: To make a classic Sea Breeze, use equal parts grapefruit and cranberry juice with the vodka.

Brain Eraser

How to repay those long hours parents work so their kids' heads can be crammed with facts? By wiping out those facts as fast as possible, of course. This drink is a perpetual adolescent, caught somewhere between a grown-up Black Russian and a childish Egg Cream. Even so, it can be fun.

1 ounce vodka
1 ounce coffee liqueur
1/2 ounce amaretto
Club soda, chilled

Combine vodka and liqueurs in a mixing glass with cracked ice. Stir and strain into a cocktail glass. Top with a layer of cold club soda. The collegiate way to drink this is through a straw that reaches all the way to the bottom, taking the spirits first. The idea is that the club soda, which is drunk last, will act as a kind of refreshing chaser.

CAVALCADE OF STUPIDITY: COLLEGE FADS

1939: SWALLOWING GOLDFISH. And this was *before* sushi bars were popular.

1952: PANTY RAIDS. On a crisp March evening at the University of Michigan, six hundred male students storm a female dorm and seize all the lingerie they can get their hands on. Soon, college men across America are conducting similar raids. The fad lasted until the

1960s, when coeds' penchant for publicly burning their bras took the thrill out of the sport.

1959: TELEPHONE-BOOTH STUFFING. You'd think a fad this nutty would have to be American, but the honor goes to South Africa, where it was known as Telephone Booth Squash. According to the rules, the booth had to remain upright, but the door could be open and only half of each participant had to be inside the booth. South Africa set a high initial standard by cramming twenty-five students into a booth, though England came in a close second with nineteen. The American record went to a group of students from St. Mary's College in California, which wedged twenty-two people into a booth. The fad died out quickly but came back briefly in the form of Volkswagen stuffing in the early 1970s.

1973: GLASS EATING. You'd think a Harvard student would have more sense, but after going out with friends one night, an undergrad showed his smarts by unscrewing a lightbulb and eating it. Eager to show their ability to think for themselves, others followed suit. The fad ended abruptly when universities, worried about the long lines at student health centers, outlawed glass as a food choice.

1974: STREAKING. Not surprisingly, this fad began in the warmer climates, first appearing at universities in Florida and Southern California. In Hawaii, a politically minded flasher streaked through the state legislature to promote the impeachment of President Nixon.

1978: TOGA PARTIES. Inspired by *National Lampoon's Animal House,* thousands of college students began wrapping themselves in sheets and calling it fun. The largest fest was held at the University of Wisconsin, where 10,000 students created 20,000 pounds of laundry in a single night.

SHOTS AND SHOOTERS

Shots have always been popular with those in search of a swift and unsophisticated sledgehammer blow to the brain, making them perfect for college youth. Dedicated to the premise that the quicker one gets drunk the quicker one can throw up, pass out, and call it a day, shooters by and large are favored by those who lack the courage to taste what they are drinking or the palate to appreciate it.

Throughout the 1980s, shooters were especially popular, and virtually every type of cocktail was re-created in a shooter version, with not necessarily happy results. More often, you'll wonder what all the fuss was about. Here are some classic campus shooters.

Mr. Braddock (William Daniels): Would you mind telling me, then, what were those four years of college for? What was the point of all that hard work?
Ben (Dustin Hoffman): Beats me.
— The Graduate, 1967

Jello Shots

Favored by those on the cusp of delayed (very delayed) adolescence who don't know if they want a Popsicle or a real drink.

1 package flavored gelatin dessert
1 cup boiling water
1 cup vodka

Add boiling water to gelatin and stir to dissolve. Let cool to room temperature. Add vodka, pour into a pan or tray, and freeze until firm.

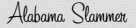

Alabama Slammer

Like all mixed drinks, this shooter should be sipped immediately.

3 ounces whiskey
1 1/2 ounces amaretto
1 1/2 ounces sloe gin
Dash of orange juice or lemon juice

Place ingredients into a shaker with ice cubes, shake, and strain into four shot glasses.

84

Peppermint Patty

1/2 ounce peppermint schnapps
1/2 ounce vodka
1/2 ounce coffee liqueur
1/2 ounce dark crème de cacao

Pour ingredients into a shaker with ice. Shake and strain into a shot glass.

Grasshopper Shot

1 ounce crème de menthe
1 ounce white crème de cacao
1 ounce heavy cream

Pour ingredients in a cocktail shaker with ice. Shake and strain into two shot glasses.

Sweet Tart

1 ounce vodka
Dash raspberry liqueur
Dash pineapple juice
Dash lime juice

Add all ingredients into a shaker with ice.
Shake and strain into a shot glass.
VARIATION: PURPLE HOOTER.
Use equal parts vodka and raspberry
liqueur, add a dash of sweet-and-sour mix
and a dash of lemon-lime soda.

Brave Bull

1 ½ ounces coffee liqueur
1 ½ ounces tequila

Place liqueur and tequila in
a cocktail shaker with plenty
of ice. Shake and strain into
two shot glasses.

Watermelon Shot

1 ounce vodka
1 ounce melon liqueur
1 ounce cranberry
juice

Place vodka, liqueur,
and cranberry juice in a
cocktail shaker with ice.
Shake and strain into
two shot glasses.

HOW TO MAKE A SHOOTER

Technically speaking, a shooter and a shot are not the same style drink, although we see the term *shooter* applied to any shot-style drink with increasing frequency. A properly made shooter is a layered drink and is the modern version of a far older-style drink, the Pousse Café, or "coffee pusher," which was popular in the 1930s. Where a Pousse Café is a layered cocktail, a shooter is its diminutive version, a layered shot. Popular among twentysomethings throughout the 1980s, a well-made shooter can be a delight.

There's no reason to be intimidated by mixing a shooter — just make sure your ingredients are of varying degrees of heaviness and pour in the order given. To avoid blending, pour each additional layer over the back of a spoon held just above the surface of the drink.

When creating your own drinks, look for ingredients of varied heaviness that will create a pleasant contrast of colors. The list below ranks selected spirits and liqueurs from heaviest to lightest, and your layers will work better if ingredients fall more than three ranks away from each other on the list.

Crème de cassis (heaviest)

Crème de cacao

Kahlúa

Peach schnapps

Crème de banane

Anisette

Crème de menthe (green)

Crème de cacao (white)

Melon liqueur

Tia Maria

Cherry brandy

Apricot brandy

Sambuca

Galliano

Amaretto

Drambuie

Benedictine

Peppermint schnapps

Frangelico

Irish cream liqueur

Cointreau

Grand Marnier

Sloe gin

Southern Comfort

Chartreuse

Ouzo

Pernod (lightest)

B-52 Shooter

It takes some skill to master the layering technique required for this shooter, but it's well worth the effort. If your layers aren't crisp, letting the drink stand a moment will give the heavier layers time to settle.

Coffee liqueur
Irish cream liqueur
Grand Marnier

Layer equal parts of each liqueur in a shot glass in the order given (heaviest to lightest).

White Spider Shooter

You won't see the layers in this white-on-white drink, but you'll taste them. The pleasure is tasting the sharp sting of the crème de menthe through the sweeter crème de cacao.

$3/_4$ ounce white crème de menthe
$3/_4$ ounce white crème de cacao

Pour crème de menthe in a shot glass; layer with crème de cacao.

Blue Moon Shooter

$1/_2$ ounce amaretto
$1/_2$ ounce Irish creme liqueur
$1/_2$ ounce blue curaçao

Layer into a shot glass.
VARIATION: BLUE POPPER.
Replace amaretto and Irish cream liqueur with 1 ounce of tequila and top with blue curaçao.

Blow Job Shooter

There are many versions of this shooter. The one below, a layered and abbreviated Black Russian, is simple and delicious.

1 ounce coffee liqueur
1 ounce vodka
Whipped cream

Pour coffee liqueur into a shot glass, and then pour in vodka. Top with whipped cream. Traditionally, this is to be drunk without using your hands.

Mod Martinis

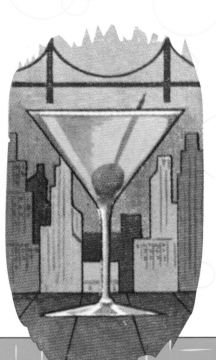

Without a doubt, Martinis, which James Bond sipped regularly, were a large part of the Cold War era — and almost every era before and after. They are the anchor of the cocktail galaxy and, save for a brief period during the fern bar era, have always been so ubiquitous they deserve a section wholly their own.

Though the Martini dates back well over a century, it is never exactly the same from one decade to the next. Each generation puts its own stamp on it, remaking the drink with every era. The Original Martini had a gin-to-dry vermouth ratio of 1:1. By the 1940s, there was twice as much gin as vermouth in the drink, and there was three times as much gin just a decade later. The contemporary Martini often contains the barest whisper of vermouth, in ratios too small to measure. To purists it may not be a Martini at all, since it is almost as likely to be made with vodka as gin. The vodka-based version was originally called a Kangaroo, and later a Vodkatini, but neither of these appellations caught on. Today, a Martini is made with gin, and its popular cousin is known simply as a Vodka Martini.

Modern Dry Martini

2½ ounces gin
1 tablespoon dry vermouth

Mix with cracked ice in a mixing glass, then strain into a chilled cocktail glass. Garnish with a stuffed olive or a twist of lemon peel.

The Nixon Martini

Bebe Rebozo — businessman, confidante, and scandal pal — used to make this version for the late President Richard Nixon. Rebozo called this an In and Out Martini, in tribute to the fleeting presence of the vermouth.

2½ ounces gin
1¾ teaspoon dry vermouth

Fill a mixing glass with cracked ice. Add vermouth, swirl the glass once, and strain off the vermouth. Add gin, stir, and strain into a chilled cocktail glass. Garnish with an olive.

The Buñuel Martini

The late Spanish filmmaker Luis Buñuel, director of *Un chien andalou, The Discreet Charm of the Bourgeoisie, That Obscure Object of Desire,* and other classics, was a Martini maven par excellence. So important was this life-sustaining cocktail that Buñuel included his personal recipe for it in *My Last Sigh,* his 1983 autobiography. Buñuel's technique, "the fruit of long experimentation," produces stunning and exceedingly satisfying results.

- The day before you plan to mix the drinks, place all ingredients — gin, vermouth, glasses, and cocktail shaker — in the refrigerator. Leave them there until the moment you are ready to mix the drink.

- Make sure your ice is very cold — at least -4° F (-30° C).

- To mix, place ice into the chilled shaker. Pour a few drops of Noilly Prat vermouth and a half a demitasse spoon of Angostura bitters over the ice. Shake, then strain off, leaving only the ice in the shaker.

- Now add gin. English gin, such as Bombay or Tanqueray, is preferred. Shake gently and strain into chilled glasses.

- Garnish with a stuffed green olive.

FAMOUS MARTINI DRINKERS

SHERWOOD ANDERSON: Martinis were his downfall. After choking on the toothpick that held the olive, he developed peritonitis and died.

HUMPHREY BOGART: His last words were, "I should never have switched from Scotch to Martinis."

LUIS BUÑUEL He once claimed that the Dry Martini had played a "very primordial role" in his life.

SOMERSET MAUGHAM: According to him, the drink should "be stirred, not shaken, so that the molecules lie sensuously on top of one another."

HERMAN WOUK: Trust a novelist to get it right. He described the Martini as "a cold cloud."

RICHARD NIXON: According to rumor, he sipped a Martini the night he announced his resignation. We can neither confirm nor deny.

HAWKEYE PIERCE: In *M*A*S*H*, he claimed that "the only green vegetables I get are Martini olives."

JAMES BOND: A vodka man, most definitely, and shaken, never stirred.

SHAKEN OR STIRRED?

Many people order their Martinis "Shaken, not stirred" for the simple — if fleeting — pleasure of pretending they are James Bond as they repeat one of his most memorable lines. They do so at their own peril. Although it may seem a trifling matter to the uninitiated, there are real differences between a Martini that is stirred and one that is shaken, and Martini purists insist that stirring is the only acceptable method of mixing this drink.

Shaking a Martini, like beating egg whites, incorporates air into the drink — the infamous sin of "bruising" the gin, which alters the taste. Shaking also does a more thorough job of dissolving the vermouth, which makes for a less oily feeling on the tongue but also gives the drink an undesirably cloudy appearance. A true classic Martini should be as clear as glass.

So was the world's coolest spy guilty of gaucherie? Was he so unhinged by facing down the infamous Dr. No that he transposed the words "shaken" and "stirred"? Not necessarily. We know from the Vesper he ordered in *Casino Royale* that Bond was a vodka enthusiast.

At other times, he ordered a "Medium Vodka Dry Martini." In a true Martini (i.e., one that is made with gin), the key concern is to avoid ruining the delicate gin by bruising, over-mixing, or similar rough handling. Vodka is a far heartier spirit and not as easily damaged. Moreover, the key concern in a Vodka Martini is to achieve the coldest possible temperature. Shaking a cocktail produces a colder drink than stirring, as more of the drink tumbles over more of the ice. So Bond, in ordering his Vodka Martini shaken rather than stirred, was, as usual, spot on.

It has become common in many bars to shake all Martinis, as it is a quicker mixing method and makes mass production far easier to accomplish. However, whether your cocktail should be shaken or stirred should depend on whether you are drinking a Martini made from gin or one made from vodka.

MARTINI VARIATIONS

The Classics

BUCKEYE MARTINI. Garnish with a black olive instead of a green one.

DIRTY MARTINI. Made by adding a few drops of olive brine.

GIBSON. Although the original Gibson was a 1:1 Martini with a maraschino cherry, today's Gibson is a very dry Martini garnished with a pearl cocktail onion.

GIMLET. To two ounces of gin, use half an ounce freshly squeezed lime juice. Garnish with a twist of lime peel.

VODKA GIMLET. To two ounces vodka, use half an ounce Rose's lime juice. Garnish with a wedge of lime.

GIN AND IT. This classic was, like the original Martini, made in a 1:1 ratio of gin and sweet vermouth. Today's version is far dryer — a generous splash of sweet vermouth to two ounces of gin.

Still in the Ballpark

APPLESAUCE MARTINI. Vodka and calvados in a 2:1 ratio, garnished with a thin slice of apple.

SOUR APPLE MARTINI. Vodka and sour apple schnapps in a 1:1 ratio, garnished with a maraschino cherry (optional).

BLACK-AND-WHITE MARTINI. Vanilla vodka and dark crème de cacao in a 4:1 ratio.

BLACK MARTINI. Vodka and sambuca in a 8:1 ratio.

BLUE MARTINI. Vodka and blue curaçao, garnished with a twist of lemon peel. Can be mixed in any ratio, from 1:1 to 10:1.

CAJUN MARTINI. Pepper-infused vodka and dry vermouth, garnished with a pepper-stuffed olive.

CAMPTINI. Gin and raspberry liqueur, garnished with a twist of lemon.

CHOCOLATE MARTINI. Vodka and chocolate liqueur, garnished with grated chocolate.

CRANTINI. Cranberry vodka and Cointreau, garnished with a twist of orange.

LEMON DROP MARTINI. Lemon vodka and Galliano in a 8:1 ratio, served in a sugar-rimmed glass with a splash of lemon juice and garnished with a twist of lemon peel.

MARTINI ROYALE. Vodka and raspberry liqueur, garnished with a twist of lemon.

MELON MARTINI. Vodka and melon liqueur in a 2:1 ratio, garnished with a cube of melon.

MOCHATINI. Chocolate vodka and coffee liqueur in a 5:1 ration, garnished with espresso beans.

SAKETINI. Gin or vodka, with Japanese sake replacing the vermouth.

STINGER MARTINI. Vodka and crème de menthe.

In Name Only

BACARDI MARTINI, ALSO KNOWN AS A BLACK DOG. White rum mixed with dry vermouth in a 10:1 ratio.

HENNESSY MARTINI. Hennessy cognac and fresh lemon juice garnished with a twist of lemon.

LIMÓN MARTINI. Bacardi Limón and dry vermouth to taste, garnished with a twist of lemon peel.

TEQUINI, ALSO KNOWN AS A MEXICAN MARTINI. Tequila and dry vermouth in a 3:1 ratio with a dash of bitters, garnished with a stuffed olive and a twist of lemon peel.

New Twists

Martini garnishes used to be strictly limited — a plain or pimento-stuffed olive or a twist of lemon peel for the Martini, a cocktail onion for the Gimlet. The move to innovative Martinis, however, has pushed the envelope in this area. The appropriately named Martini's Restaurant in New York City, for example, introduced anchovy- or prosciutto-stuffed olives for Gin Martinis, and olives stuffed with lemon, rosemary, or chipotle peppers for Vodka Martinis. So the next time you have a jar of olives and some time to kill, try stuffing them with tasty little tidbits — you might invent a signature garnish all your own!

Drink Index

95

Online Sources

To ensure yours is the best-dressed bar in town, may we recommend . . .

http://www.atomic-tiki.com Tiki and lounge items for your bar.

http://www.tropictreasures.com Party gear and decorations for the tiki- and tropical-minded.

http://www.surlatable.com A particularly comprehensive assortment of basics and accessories, from shakers and bar sets to cocktail charms and flamingo glasses.

For history and recipes, as well as to keep abreast of the spirit world, we suggest sites hosted by your favorite spirits manufacturer. Check out some of the following:

> http://www.absolut.com
> http://www.bacardi.com
> http://www.bartender.com
> http://www.midoriworld.com
> http://www.plymouthgin.com
> http://www.seagram.com
> http://www.smirnoff.com
> http://www.straightbourbon.com